Syndicated Lending

Essential Capital Markets

Books in the series:

Cash Flow Forecasting
Corporate Valuation
Credit Risk Management
Finance of International Trade
Mergers and Acquisitions
Portfolio Management in Practice
Project Finance
Syndicated Lending

Syndicated Lending

Andrew Fight

ELSEVIER
BUTTERWORTH
HEINEMANN

AMSTERDAM • BOSTON • HEIDELBERG • LONDON • NEW YORK • OXFORD
PARIS • SAN DIEGO • SAN FRANCISCO • SINGAPORE • SYDNEY • TOKYO

Elsevier Butterworth-Heinemann
Linacre House, Jordan Hill, Oxford OX2 8DP
30 Corporate Drive, Burlington, MA 01803

Copyright © 2004, Andrew Fight. All rights reserved

Note

The materials contained in this book remain the copyrighted intellectual property of Andrew Fight, are destined for use in his consulting activities, and are to be clearly identified as copyrighted to him.

Andrew Fight has asserted his right under the Copyrights, Designs, and Patents Act 1988, to be identified as author of this work, and confirms that he retains ownership of the intellectual property and rights to use these materials in his training courses and consulting activities.

No part of this publication may be reproduced in any material form (including photocopying or storing in any medium by electronic means and whether or not transiently or incidentally to some other use of this publication) without the written permission of the copyright holder except in accordance with the provisions of the Copyright, Designs, and Patents Act 1998 or under the terms of a licence issued by the Copyright Licensing Agency Ltd, 90 Tottenham Court Road, London, England W1T 4LP. Applications for the copyright holder's written permission to reproduce any part of this publication should be addressed to the publisher

Permissions may be sought directly from Elsevier's Science and Technology Rights Department in Oxford, UK: phone: (+44) (0) 1865 843830; fax: (+44) (0) 1865 853333; e-mail: permissions@elsevier.co.uk. You may also complete your request on-line via the Elsevier homepage (www.elsevier.com), by selecting 'Customer Support' and then 'Obtaining Permissions'

British Library Cataloguing in Publication Data
A catalogue record for this book is available from the British Library

Library of Congress Cataloguing in Publication Data
A catalogue record for this book is available from the Library of Congress

ISBN 0 7506 5907 6

> For information on all Elsevier Butterworth-Heinemann finance publications visit our website at http://books.elsevier.com/finance

Composition by Charon Tec Pvt. Ltd, Chennai, India

Transferred to digital printing in 2008.

Contents

Foreword		**ix**
1	**Introduction to syndicated loans**	**1**
	What is a syndicated loan?	1
	The growth of the syndicated loan market	2
	The secondary market in syndicated loans	6
2	**Attractions of the syndicated loan market**	**7**
	The borrower	7
	The participants	12
	The arranger and the agent	19
	Tombstones	22
	Syndications timetable – from mandate to drawdown	25
	Exercise 1	26
	Answers to Exercise 1	27
3	**Responsibilities and obligations of syndicated loan participants**	**29**
	The borrower	29
	How the borrower chooses an arranger for the syndicated loan	31
	The participants and their responsibilities	33
	Other considerations affecting participants in a syndicated loan	36

	Roles of the arranger and the agent	37
	Exercise 2	40
	Answers to Exercise 2	41
4	**The major players in the syndicated loans market**	**43**
	League tables	43
	Barclays Capital	63
5	**Structures used in syndicated loans**	**66**
	Overview of syndications	66
	Term of loan	67
	Revolving facilities	68
	Committed and uncommitted facilities	68
	Single currency or multi-currency	69
	Repayment profiles	69
	Repayments via bond issues/acquisition finance	70
	Evergreen facilities	72
	Senior debt, mezzanine finance, and subordinated loans	73
	A subordinated loan	73
	Securitization	74
	Trade finance/pre-export finance	75
	Stock loans	76
	Project finance	77
	Aircraft finance	82
	Ship construction finance	83
	Non-recourse loans	83
	Standby credits	83
	Property finance	84
	Vodafone AirTouch	85
6	**The Loan agreement**	**89**
	The preamble	90
	Definitions	91
	The facility	96
	Purpose	96
	Conditions precedent	97
	Utilization	98

Repayment	98
Prepayment	100
Interest rate	101
Fees	103
Taxes and other deductions	105
Other indemnities	105
Guarantee	106
Representations and warranties	108
Undertakings	110
Indemnities	114
Currency	115
The agent and lenders	115
Sharing payments	116
Transfers of participations	116
Changes to the obligors	119
Waivers, amendments, and consents	120
Partial invalidity	120
Governing law and jurisdiction	121
Legal opinions	121
7 Loan covenants	**125**
The function of loan covenants	125
Types of covenants	129
Negotiating the covenants in the loan agreement	132
Functioning of covenants during the loan	137
Breach of covenant	140
Other issues	143
8 Secondary loan markets	**146**
History and development of the secondary loan market	146
LSTA	149
LMA	153
Syndicated loans and credit rating agencies	156
Glossary	**168**
Index	**183**

Foreword

Welcome to this book on syndicated loans.

This book is presented in nine chapters, each of which treats a specific part of the syndicated lending process. The individual chapters cover the following topics:

- Introduction to syndicated loans
- Attractions of the syndicated loan market
- Responsibilities and obligations of syndicated loan participants
- The major players in the syndicated loans market
- Structures used in syndicated loans
- The loan agreement
- Loan covenants
- Secondary loan markets
- Glossary.

This book aims to explain the background and raison d'être of the syndicated Loan as one of the mechanisms of the capital markets to provide finance to borrowers, the players and mechanics in syndicated lending, and the various benefits and risks involved in taking part in the syndicated loan market – one of the most important activities of banks in today's worldwide market – and have a good working knowledge of the challenges and opportunities which are open to you.

Foreword

We believe that this book Introduction to Syndicated Lending, will be informative and instructional, and an indispensable aid to persons seeking to understand the syndicated loans market.

Andrew Fight
www.andrewfight.com

Chapter 1

Introduction to syndicated loans

What is a syndicated loan?

A syndicated loan is a loan which is provided to the borrower by two or more banks known as participants, which is governed by a single loan agreement. The loan is arranged and structured by an arranger, and managed by an agent. The arranger and the agent may also be participants. Each participant provides a defined percentage of the loan, and receives the same percentage of repayments.

The syndicated lending market is international by nature – that is to say, many of the borrowers and projects being financed are international – taking place in Europe, Eastern Europe, Africa, the Middle East, etc. Furthermore, in order to place these large loans (e.g. up to several hundred million dollars) in the market, sometimes several banks are needed to participate in these loans.

The factors which account for the size and spectacular growth of this market are several:

- The market is international rather than being confined to a particular country, and new debt issues can avoid a great deal of national regulation which may involve onerous registration requirements. This can lead to a significant reduction in the cost of the issue.
- The international syndicated lending market has evolved a very fast, efficient, and flexible distribution network which can place deals in large volumes and for the most part can ensure that they are launched successfully and in an orderly fashion.

- This is because syndicated loans are managed, underwritten, and sold by syndicates. These syndicates are dominated by the London-based Swiss, American, European, and Japanese banks which have access to large client bases.
- The international marketplace gives borrowers access to a greater number and diversity of investors than would be possible within their own marketplace. This ability to tap different sources of finance can reduce overall interest costs.
- The most important European banking markets are based in the UK. The effect of London being the UK's capital city should not be over-estimated. The large volume of activities, the variety and innovation of banking products, the large number of people employed in the UK banking industry is significantly influenced by the strength of the London trading and capital market activities.

The growth of the syndicated loan market

The syndicated loan market was initially developed in London by a relatively small number of merchant banks which had small balance sheets but large and important customers. It would not have been possible for these merchant banks to provide the full amounts of loans needed by their customers, and so other banks were asked to provide parts of the loans on the same terms and conditions, with the merchant bank taking a fee to arrange the loan and administer it once it was drawn. In today's terms, the merchant bank was acting as arranger and agent.

During the 1960s many North American and other foreign banks opened branches in London, attracted by the growth of the new Eurodollar market. These new branches could gain assets quickly and easily by participating in syndicated loans to borrowers with which they would not otherwise have had a relationship. The American and Japanese banks in particular began targeting large companies with the specific intention of arranging syndicated loans in order to maximize their fee income. In recent years in the London market, the part played by Japanese banks as arrangers has lessened and some of the UK clearing banks have become increasingly active.

Introduction to syndicated loans

Today the syndicated loan market is a major part of the operations of banks throughout the world, with major centres in London, New York, and Hong Kong. They are typically used to finance large projects such as the Jorf Lasfar Power Station in Morocco – one of the largest syndicated loans.

The following table shows the amount of syndicated loans arranged globally in the years 1992–2003. It shows that the total amounts raised

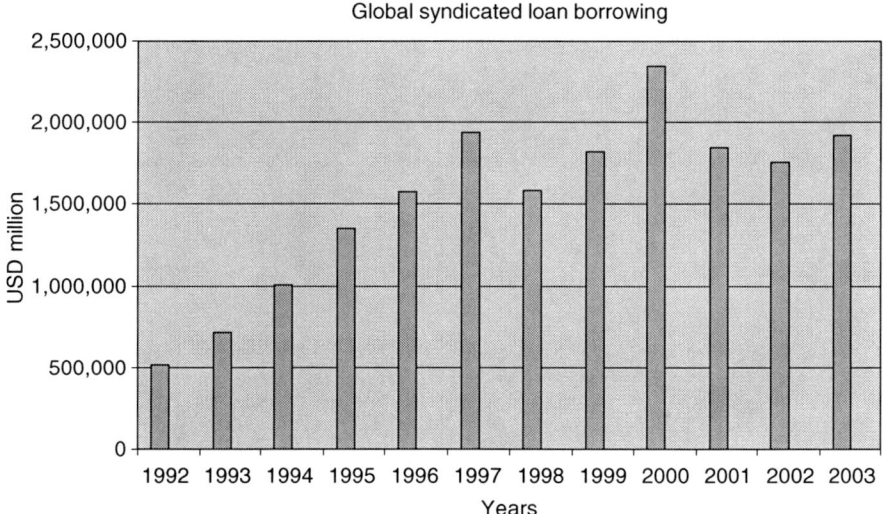

Source: Dealogic, 2003

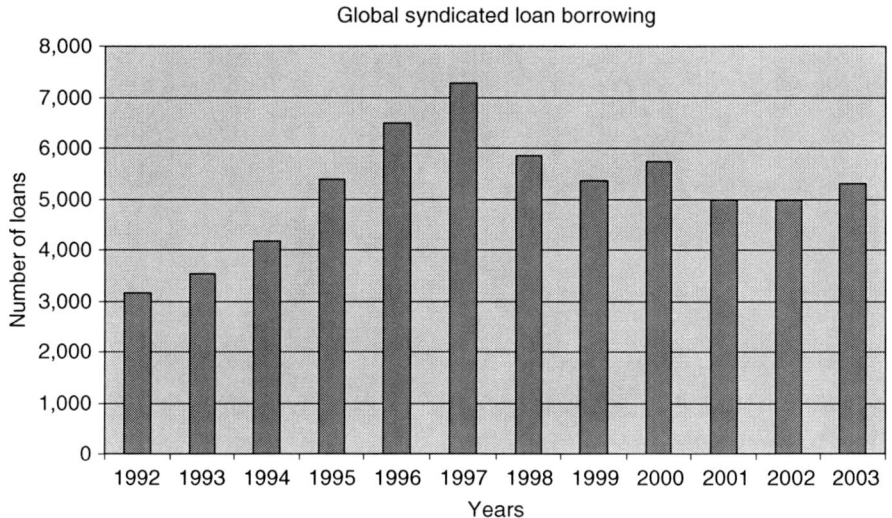

Source: Dealogic, 2003

4 Syndicated Lending

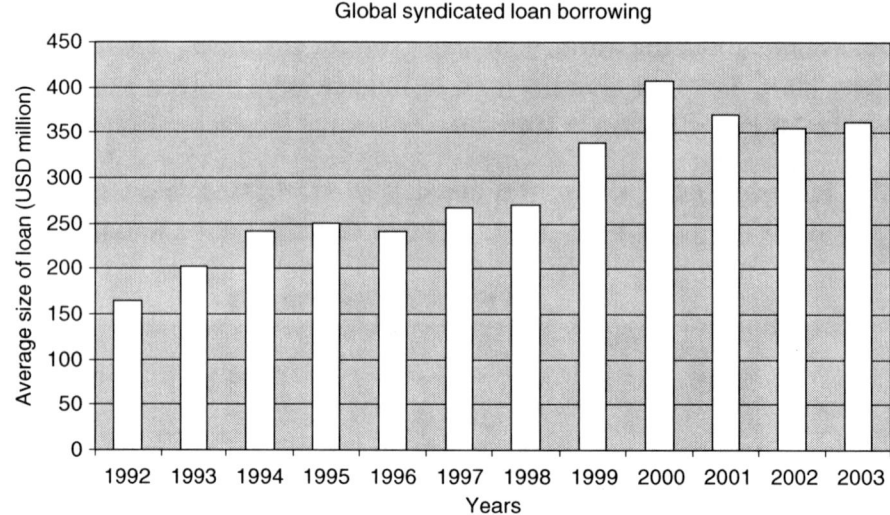

Source: Dealogic, 2003

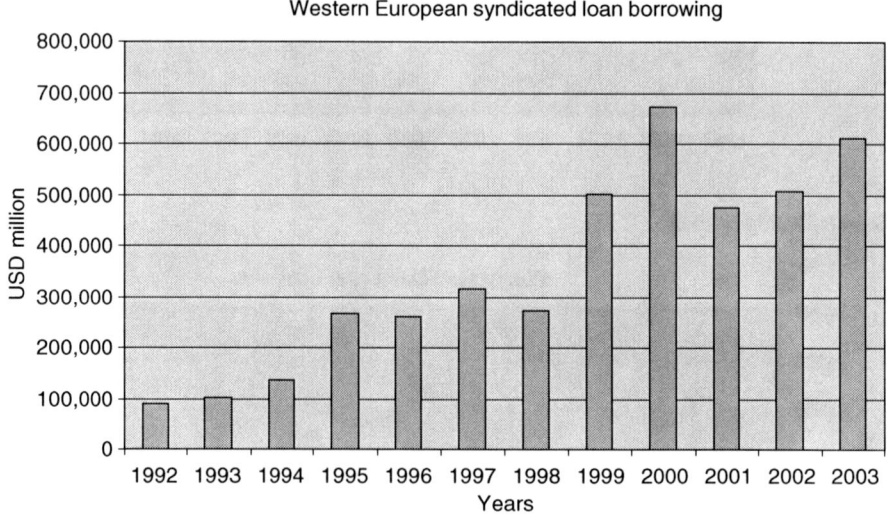

Source: Dealogic, 2003

annually has more than tripled during this period, despite the fact that the number of individual loans has slipped back over the last 3 years.

The average size of individual loans has increased steadily throughout the period, from USD 155 mn in 1992 to USD 350 mn in 2003.

Introduction to syndicated loans

For example, during 2000 two 'jumbo' loans of Euros 30 bn each were finalized in favour of Vodafone plc and France Telecom.

The attraction of the syndicated loans market to borrowers worldwide can be seen by comparing the above global table with that of syndicated

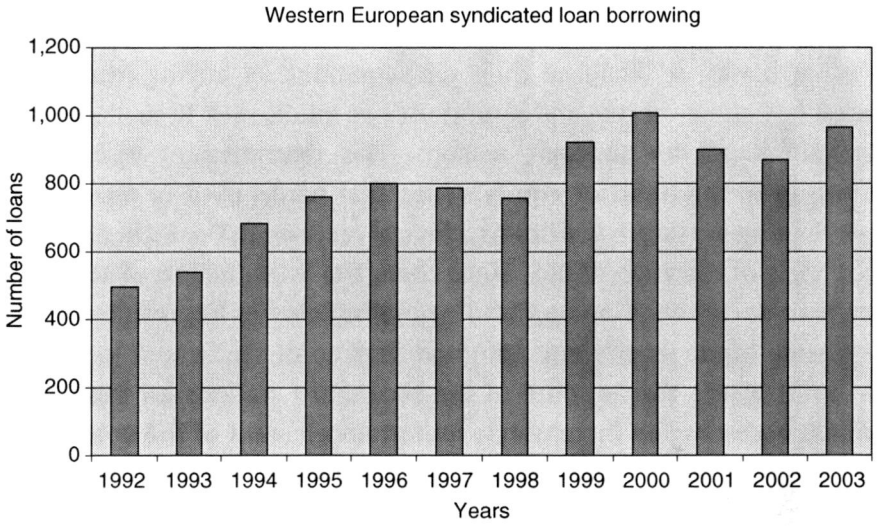

Source: Dealogic, 2003

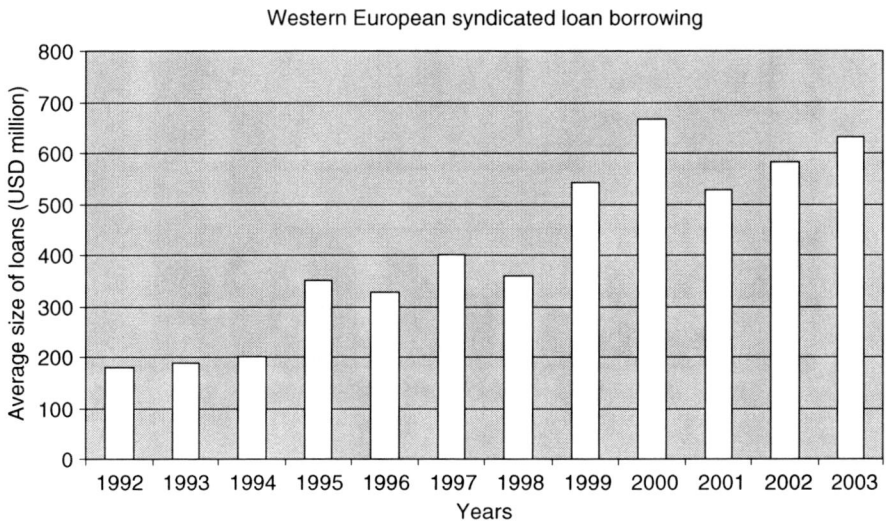

Source: Dealogic, 2003

loans made to Western European borrowers. Similar growth is witnessed in both categories.

The secondary market in syndicated loans

In the mid-1990s, a secondary market in syndicated loans (i.e. a market in which participants can sell all or part of their existing participations to other banks, or increase their participations by buying from other banks) has grown in size and importance as banks seek to manage their portfolio levels for strategic reasons. This development is a logical follow-up to the debt for equity swaps that banks used to reconfigure their lending portfolios which was a logical reaction to the Latin American debt crisis of the early 1980s. Since then, the introduction of standardized loan documentation and trading methodologies has resulted in the increasing homogeneity and commoditization of syndicated loans – to the point where the appetite of the secondary markets for syndicated loans is becoming an increasingly important element of the syndication strategy for syndicated loans. This development is discussed in further detail in Chapter 8.

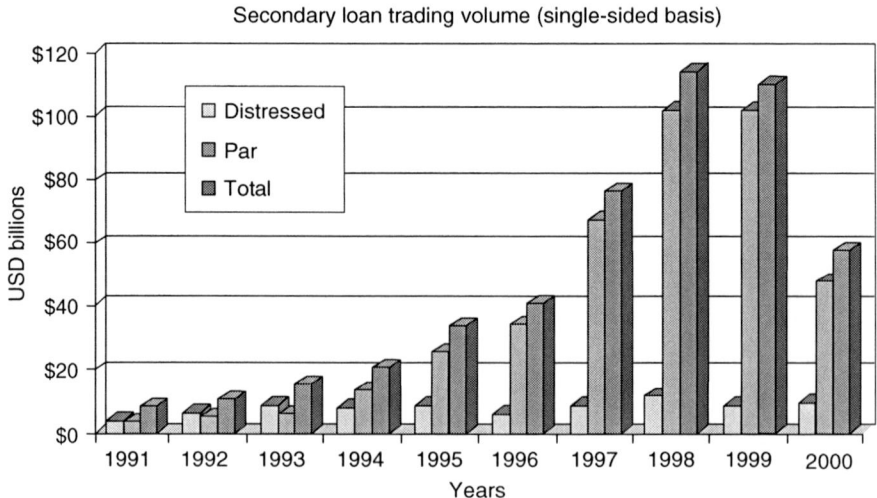

Source: LSTA

Chapter 2

Attractions of the syndicated loan market

The syndicated loans market exists because there are attractions and benefits to each of the parties involved.

These are described as follows from the viewpoints of the various participating parties.

The borrower

Ability to arrange cross border transactions

The borrower need not be resident in the country in which the loan is arranged, so long as it does not breach any law or regulation (e.g. withholding tax or foreign currency restrictions) in its country of residence. It can therefore avoid any domestic funding constraints which may exist in its home market, and make new relationships with banks from different countries.

Alternate borrowers/Special Purpose Vehicles

The borrowing company may choose to use a particular subsidiary as the borrower under the terms of the loan agreement, such as an existing subsidiary company (in which case the holding company or the main trading company may have to guarantee the borrower).

In certain circumstances a borrowing company may use a 'Special Purpose Vehicle' (SPV), which is a new company formed solely for the purpose of funding this loan and receiving income to be used in repayment of the loan. The SPV will have no assets or liabilities apart from its issued capital, and may be legally unrelated to the borrowing company seeking the syndicated loan.

Income received by the borrowing company and intended to be used in the repayment of the loan will usually be 'ring-fenced', i.e. legally separated from other funds so that they are not available for any other purposes.

This type of structure will normally be used only for specialized transactions for a well regarded company, as banks making a credit assessment of the proposal will have to consider whether or not the borrower may be viewed on a 'stand alone' basis, knowing that the loan will be repaid only from the proceeds of the underlying transaction and without recourse to the parent company of the SPV.

Structure and purpose of loan

Banks in London and other major financial centres have considerable experience in assessing many different types of loan, and syndicated loans can be arranged for a wide variety of purposes.

The arranger can be extremely useful to the borrower in advising on the structure which would be acceptable to the overall banking market, and the margin and fees which the participants would expect to receive.

Restriction of negotiation

The borrower usually deals with only one bank, the arranger, in negotiating the terms and conditions of the syndicated loan, rather than having separate discussions with a large number of different banks. It also minimizes its accounting functions by receiving one payment from the agent when the loan is drawn and making only one payment to the agent when repayment is due.

Uniform terms and conditions

Only one set of loan documentation is used in a syndicated loan, signed by the borrower, the agent and all the participants. The borrower can therefore be certain that all the banks providing the loan have done so under the same conditions and with the same covenants.

It can also be assured that, so long as these conditions and covenants are not breached, a single bank cannot suddenly and unreasonably decide to ask for repayment. If security for the loan is given, the benefit is shared between the banks in the same percentage as their loan participations, and this can prevent one bank from realizing its own security (e.g. calling a guarantee) in haste so as to gain a timing advantage over other banks if the borrower should fall into difficulties.

Speed of finalization

As the borrower deals only with the arranger, which is responsible for supplying information on the borrower to potential participants in a form which the arranger is confident will satisfy their credit approval requirements, the loan can be marketed and finalized in a much shorter time frame than if the borrower were dealing with a larger number of banks.

If the transaction is very large and speed (and perhaps confidentiality) are of the essence, the borrower may arrange for the loan to be underwritten by a small number of banks which will provide the whole amount of the loan between them with the intention of subsequently launching the loan in the general syndicated loan market and reducing their participations to a lower level.

Other mechanisms available to a borrower for raising large amounts of funds, such as the bond market or raising new capital from shareholders by an equity issue, require far higher amounts of disclosure, may require the borrower to obtain a rating from rating agencies such as Moody's or Standard & Poor's, may be delayed by a queuing system as is used in the bond market, and are therefore likely to take much longer to complete (as well as incurring higher legal and accountancy fees). A borrower is therefore likely to prefer to go to the syndicated loan market.

It still remains possible for the borrower to arrange that repayment of the loan will be made from a future bond issue or equity issue.

Effect on margins and fees

The arranger supplies potential participants with an information memorandum which is designed to give the potential participant all the information it requires to make a decision on whether or not to participate in the loan. The information memorandum will contain background data of the borrower and its business activities, audited accounts of the borrower, an explanation of the purpose of the loan, details of the repayment schedule and how repayments will be achieved, an outline of the terms and conditions of the loan, etc.

The information memorandum is prepared by the arranger in consultation with the borrower, and is designed to fill all the requirements of the potential participant in making a credit decision on whether or not to join the syndicated loan. This makes it relatively quick and simple for the potential participant – it should not need to undertake independent inquiries into the credit standing of the borrower and the likelihood of timely repayment being made.

In addition, financial information such as audited annual accounts and unaudited 6 monthly management accounts, confirmation that none of the financial covenants have been breached, and any other information which may affect the repayment of the syndicated loan, will be distributed by the agent to the participants periodically in future by the agent so that participants can carry out annual reviews of the syndicated loan. These factors make it relatively easy, inexpensive and less time consuming for a bank to participate, and it can therefore be prepared to accept a lower overall return (made up of interest margin and fees) than would otherwise be likely. This obviously lowers the overall cost of borrowing to the borrower.

Bilateral relationships with participants

A borrower may have only a limited number of existing banking relationships; or it may have a number of facilities which it struggles to utilize but which it does not wish to lose because of under-utilization. The use of a syndicated loan facility can enable a borrower to overcome both these problems.

The borrower is relying upon the arranger to bring a number of banks into the syndicate. It is likely that the borrower will not have an existing relationship with the majority of these banks. Although the syndicated loan will satisfy the particular needs of the borrower for the purpose of the loan, it is possible that a number of the 'new' banks will, now that they know the borrower, be prepared to offer other facilities on a bilateral basis.

This is particularly true if a loan has been oversubscribed – e.g. if the borrower had been seeking to raise GBP 100 mn but the arranger has received positive responses totalling GBP 120 mn – in this case the borrower has the option of accepting the increased amount or not. In the latter case the participants will be 'scaled back' and their participations will be reduced so that the total loan remains at GBP 100 mn. Participants will then be faced with lending a lower amount than their credit committees have authorized. Even if the syndicated loan is not oversubscribed, a bank may be offered a participation which is lower than it would be prepared to risk on this borrower. Or there may be overseas subsidiaries of the borrower in the country of residence of the head office of a participant, where a new funding relationship, or perhaps a foreign exchange or derivative facility, could be helpful to the borrower.

Thus there can be valid opportunities for the borrower to make new banking relationships, for present and for future needs, and opportunities for the participants to maximize their returns from this new connection.

In the case of the borrower which has collected more bilateral facilities from various banks than it can regularly use, it can ensure that the arranger invites those banks into the syndicated loan. The borrower can thus protect a relationship which may otherwise wither away from under-utilization, and it can also convert what was possibly an uncommitted short-term facility into a committed medium- or long-term loan.

Market presence

The successful completion of a syndicated loan serves as a marker for a borrower, and the fact that it has raised a specified amount in this market is recorded not only by banks but also by specialist financial magazines. Potential participants will often check back to see what amounts a borrower has previously raised, and an established borrower with a good past record can find it easier to raise new amounts.

The participants

Simplicity and speed

In an era in which banks compete to maximize earnings and minimize costs, the syndicated loan offers an opportunity to gain assets in a relatively quick and simple way. The potential participant is contacted by the arranger and, once it has shown outline interest in the proposal, it is provided with the information memorandum which provides virtually all the information the bank requires to make a credit decision.

The time allotted for the credit decision is normally 2 or 3 weeks. If that decision is positive the bank will commit itself for a specific maximum participation subject to the documentation being satisfactory. It then receives the draft documentation, with a further week or so being allowed for approval or comments. The table on page 25 illustrates a typical loan syndications timetable.

The loan agreement will be signed shortly thereafter, the agent will notify the participants that all conditions precedent have been met, and drawdown can then be made. The whole process can therefore be carried out in a short period of time and is designed to make it as easy as possible for the participant to complete. Similarly, information on the financial condition of the borrower, such as the audited annual accounts and 6 monthly unaudited management accounts, will be provided to the participants by the agent as one of the conditions of the loan agreement, together with regular statements showing that no financial covenants have been breached and reports showing the progress the borrower is making towards repayment. This information is important for the participant's annual reviews of the loan while it remains outstanding.

Reduced need for direct marketing

It is not suggested that a bank should not engage in direct marketing, or that the syndicated loans market will provide enough business to fill a bank's loan portfolio. However it does mean that the bank does not have to rely only upon its own marketing efforts, and that its marketing team and the related expenses of that team can be kept to a minimum.

Quality and spread of assets

The London branch of a foreign bank can find that although its parent bank is important in its own region or country of residence, in London it is only one of over 600 banks seeking new business. It can easily find that a finance director or corporate treasurer of a company is simply not interested in meeting its representatives because of time constraints or because the company already has ample banking relationships for its day-to-day requirements.

Conversely, a sizeable company may be happy to deal with the bank but only at a level that is in excess of the size of facility which the bank is prepared to grant. The branch may therefore be tempted to take on a lower quality of business, or find that it can only attract business connected with its parent bank's country of residence, simply because it cannot obtain the domestic business which would be ideal for the branch. Participations in syndicated loans can remove this cause for concern. The branch can begin a relationship with the borrower at relatively low percentage of the total syndicated loan, and subsequently increase its exposure if it chooses to do so.

Another possibility is that the branch or bank may have specialized knowledge and a good customer base in particular sectors of business (e.g. trade finance) but a lesser developed first hand knowledge and lack of contacts in other sectors (e.g. property lending or project finance). As long as it has the skills properly to assess the risks in the latter categories, it can build assets in these sectors through participations in the syndicated loan market and thereby gain a healthy spread of asset sectors across its loan portfolio and avoid a strategically unhealthy concentration of assets on particular sectors or borrowers. Through dealings in the secondary market for syndicated loans (which is dealt with in more detail in Chapter 8) the bank can assess the overall content of its loan portfolio from time to time and buy new assets or sell existing assets in order to manage the spread of its loan portfolio.

In today's climate of mergers and acquisitions of banks, this ability to manage a loan portfolio for strategic reasons is particularly important; if the loan portfolios of two banks are merged, there may well be an overall concentration of assets by borrower, sector or country risk which needs to be adjusted. This can be done through the secondary market, either by selling existing assets or by increasing assets in a sector which would otherwise be under-represented.

Market presence

The major players in the syndicated loan market, especially those banks which aim regularly to act as arrangers or agent banks, record all syndicated loans and those banks which participate in them. In this way they are able to note which banks have a particular appetite for certain types or structures of loans, and particularly banks which show interest in certain country risks for cross-border loans. Those participants are likely to be amongst the first contacted for similar transactions in the future. A bank or branch can therefore gain market presence by being seen to be an active member of the syndicated loans market.

Regulatory pressures and capital adequacy

In 1987 the Basle agreement, under the regulatory auspices of the Bank for International Settlements, laid down certain requirements for capital adequacy of authorized banks, under which different types of loan assets are weighted according to certain standards and applied against the capital of the banks. This was agreed in order to regularize international standards and to ensure that banks do not become over-committed to particular sectors without resultant increases in the bank's capital funds, in order to maintain a minimum capital adequacy and therefore protection for depositors. Once again, operations in the syndicated loans market can enable banks to ensure that their capital adequacy ratios are maintained.

Tax efficiency

A bank or branch committing to participate in a syndicated loan is permitted to nominate a 'booking office' in a different country, from which its participation in the loan will be made. A bank may elect to do this if it is tax efficient for it to do so. For example, in the 1990s, some banks have elected to open branches in Dublin to take advantage of certain tax advantages which the government of Ireland has made available by creating an 'offshore' tax structure under which banks opening branches there face a greatly reduced tax burden on assets booked there. This reduction of tax can increase the overall return on participations in syndicated loans.

Fee income

A participant in a syndicated loan usually receives an amount of fee income as well as an interest margin.

The arranging bank typically receives a fee known as a Praecipium, which is a fee for 'opening the file' and beginning the underwriting.

This fee income usually consists of a participation fee and a commitment fee. There can sometimes also be a utilization fee, and other types of fees in more structured sectors of lending.

- The participation fee is a flat, one off-fee payable on or shortly after the date of signature of the loan agreement. It is determined according to the amount of the loan to which the bank commits; as an example, it could be that a commitment of up to GBP 5,000,000 would attract a fee

of ⅛% flat; and for amounts above GBP 5,000,000 this fee could increase to ¼% flat.
- Commitment fees are payable on the undrawn amount of the loan, and usually start to accrue either on the date of signing of the loan agreement or on a specified later date (say 30 days after the signing date). They continue to accrue until the loan is drawn down in full. If the loan is drawndown in instalments, the commitment fee will continue to accrue on the undrawn portion of the loan until the loan is fully drawn. Commitment fees are usually paid quarterly or semi-annually in arrears.
- A utilization fee may be payable on a loan where there are a number of drawdowns and is payable at or shortly after the date of each drawdown.

These fees represent off balance sheet earnings and increase the overall profitability of the transaction return on assets (ROA) to the participants.

In Tables 1 and 2, we provide a hypothetical breakdown for a fee income calculation for a loan syndication.

- In Table 1, the zones in boxes are data input zones (e.g. can be defined by the agent bank as part of the syndication strategy) and the other zones are automatically calculated in function of the loan syndication composition (data in boxes). It is assumed that the arrangers and underwriters hold a portion of their participation and syndicate the remainder to the participants. Later, they may sell or trade their retained portions on the secondary loan markets of which we shall describe later. Note that as the categories move from arranger to participant that the various fees either are reduced or disappear altogether. The actual margins over the lending rate (London Inter Bank Offered Rate, LIBOR) however remain unchanged. In other words, profitability lies not in the lending activity but in your position in the hierarchy of arranging the loan.
- Table 2 illustrates the fee calculations for a loan syndication. It immediately becomes apparent that those players involved in the structuring and syndicating of the facility obtain arrangement and underwriting fees which the simple participants do not obtain. This has the result of nearly doubling the yield (82.4 vs. 46.6) on the funds advanced.

Table 1

Yield calculations case study: 5 year fully underwritten bullet loan of EUR 500 mn

Assumptions
arranger underwrites whole amount to win mandate
Amount is sub-underwritten by two banks @ EUR 150 mn each
Banks invited into general syndication @ EUR 35 mn each and EUR 20 mn brackets
Utilization Fee assumes drawing of 100%
Copyright Andrew Fight

No of players ———>		1		2		5		10	
		Lead arranger/ Underwriter		arranger/ Sub-underwriter		Senior Lead manager		Lead manager	
Committed (U/W) Amount		500,000,000		150,000,000		35,000,000		20,000,000	
Final hold		45,000,000		40,000,000					
Maturity		5		5		5		5	
Repayment		Bullet		Bullet		Bullet		Bullet	
Margin over reference rate	bp	37.5		37.5		37.5		37.5	
Utilization Fee	bp	7.5		7.5		7.5		7.5	
Commitment Fees	bp	17.5		17.5		17.5		17.5	
Arrangement Fees (borrower)	bp	35.0							
Split									
Praecipium		10.0							
Underwriting/Sub_UW fee		10.0		10.0					
Participating fee		15.0		15.0		12.5		8.0	
		1,875,000		562,500		131,250		75,000	
		375,000		112,500		26,250		15,000	
		875,000		262,500		61,250		35,000	
		1,750,000							
		500,000		0		0		0	
		200,000		150,000		0		0	
		67,500		60,000		43,750		16,000	
Arrangement Fees per participant		767,500		210,000		43,750		16,000	
Arrangement Fees per category		767,500		420,000		218,750		160,000	
Arrangement Fees all categories		1,566,250							
Pool difference		183,750							
Pool yield – Shared as follows (ratio of allocated amount 2:1.5:1.5)									
Lead arranger	1	73,500							
Arranger	2	55,125							
		3.3							
		2.8							

Table 2

Yield (drawn) bp pa			
Retained asset	45,000,000	40,000,000	35,000,000	20,000,000
Average life (years)	5	5	5	5
Fee yield bp pa	34.1	10.5	2.5	1.6
Margin bp pa	37.5	37.5	37.5	37.5
Utilization Fee bp pa	7.5	7.5	7.5	7.5
Yield	79.1	55.5	47.5	46.6
Pool yield		3.3	2.8	
Total yield		82.4	58.3	47.5	46.6

Copyright Andrew Fight

bp pa = basis points per annum

Table 3

Syndication strategy and final hold targets

	Amount	Amount U/W	Final hold
Underwriting			
Lead arranger	1	500,000,000	500,000,000	45,000,000
Sub-underwriting arranger	2	150,000,000	300,000,000	80,000,000
General syndication				
Senior lead manager	5	35,000,000		175,000,000
Lead manager	10	20,000,000		200,000,000
Result				500,000,000

Copyright Andrew Fight

In other words, for those arranging and bringing the deal to market, the rewards are twice as profitable as for those merely participating. Ultimately, this means that the bank's ROA becomes twice as profitable.

Ascending the market hierarchy to become a market maker as opposed to market taker is therefore a primary concern of banks involved in this market, and the profits on large ticket syndicated loans can therefore be enormous.

- The third table shows the rough 'syndication strategy' of the loan so that the arranging bank has a rough idea of the number of participants and amount of their participation required for a successful syndication. This will help the bank focus on actual market characteristics and identify potential banks and categories of banks to invite into the syndication. Of course, reality differs from theory and the bank may have to reallocate portions allocated to participants.

In the case the loan is popular and more banks than expected decide to participate in the loan, the loan is said to be oversubscribed and participations are reduced (scaled back). Likewise, if the loan meets with lack of interest, it is said to be undersubscribed. In such cases, banks may be offered a larger portion than expected (sometimes welcomed by banks if the remuneration of the loan is attractive, sometimes rejected by the banks if the loan characteristics are unattractive, in which case the arranging bank will provide the shortfall).

Undersubscribed loans may be known as unsuccessful syndications, which are embarrassing to both agent bank and borrower since it indicates that either the borrower is unattractive to the markets, or that the agent bank is not sufficiently professional to understand the market to ensure a successful syndication. Such scenarios can result in lawsuits between the borrower and agent bank.

The arranger and the agent

Although the arranger and the agent fulfil different roles, it is quite normal for the arranger also to be the agent in a syndicated loan facility. The arranger negotiates and syndicates, the facility, and the agent manages the facility once the loan agreement has been signed. The arranger's role is therefore normally completed once signing takes place, but it will often wish to continue its involvement in the facility by acting as agent.

A hypothetical loan syndication is graphically depicted below.

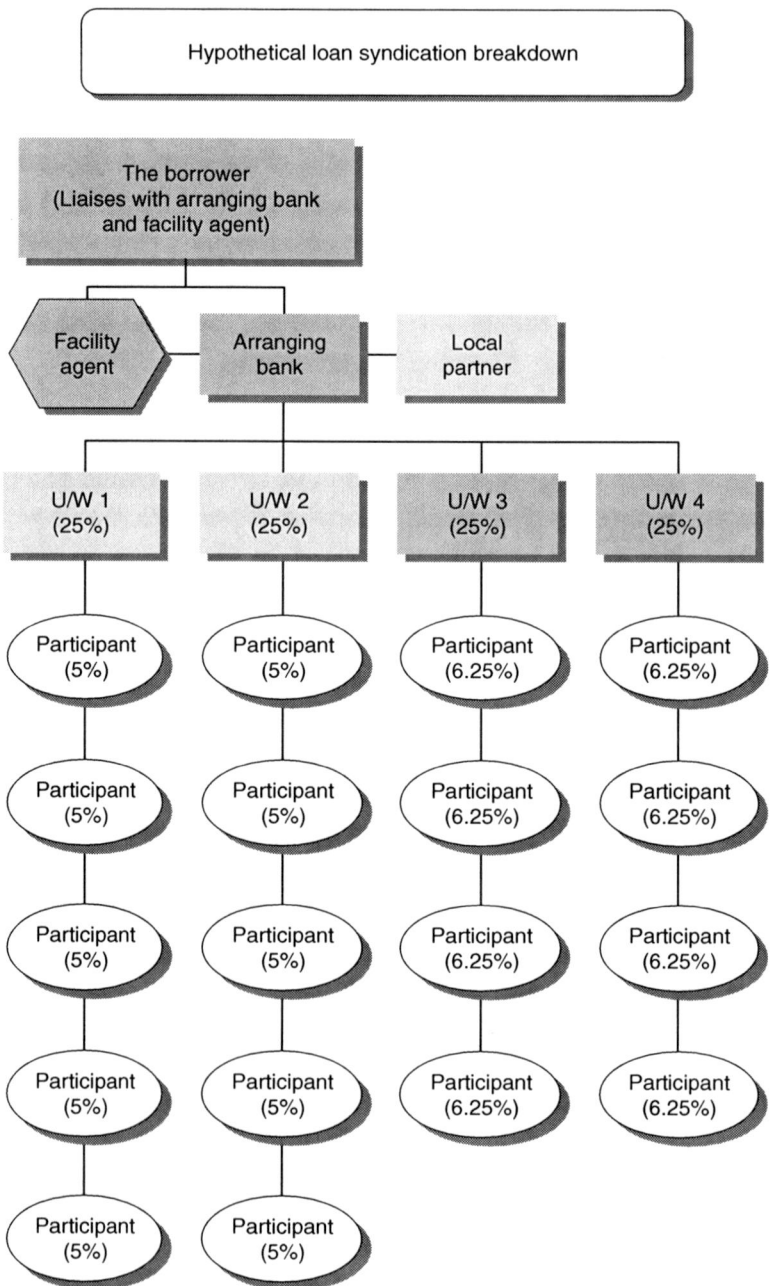

Fee income

As we saw in the previous tables, the main attraction of the roles of arranger and agent bank is the increased fee income which structuring and managing the loan will earn. The fees are negotiable with the borrower and will generally consist of a flat fee payable at or around the date of first drawdown, plus annual fees payable to the agent throughout the life of the loan.

These fees can be considerable because of the amount of work involved in the initial stages when participants are brought into the loan, and the administration workload thereafter. These fees are in addition to the fees which the agent will earn from its own participation in the syndicated loan.

Market presence

Details of most syndicated loans are published by advertisements known as 'tombstones' which are placed in national newspapers and specialist financial magazines by the arranger and which show the borrower, the amount of the syndicated loan and the names of the participants.

Annual league tables are compiled showing the total amounts of syndicated loans arranged by each bank, and success in gaining a high position in these league tables show the structuring ability and the placing power of the bank and can therefore be used in its marketing efforts to attract more mandates to arrange new loans.

Increased competition has meant that the ability of an arranger to structure a syndicated loan in an imaginative or 'groundbreaking' way has become increasingly important, especially with 'jumbo' loans which may need to be repaid (or 'taken out') by a future bond or commercial paper issue.

This can be particularly important to the borrower as this future source of repayment (which is probably not described in detail at the time of syndication) will have increased acceptance and market confidence if potential participants know that the arranger is capable of handling this type of debt issue.

Some readers may point out that depending on a loan repayment from a subsequent bond or equity issue as opposed to the classic sources of repayment from cash flow, asset conversion cycles or secured assets is at odds with classic financial analysis and prudent lending credit criteria. They will indeed be correct, but will also realize that the excessively conservative and slow reacting bank risks losing business and being left on the sidelines. The recent development of the jumbo syndicated loan being placed on the markets with the tacit understanding of a subsequent takeout by a bond or equity issue necessitates a thorough and profound understanding of the market, its dynamics, and appetite for risk, now and in the near future. It is these subjective skills which some banks are able to harness and propel themselves to the upper tiers as underwriters, and which are beyond the reach of others, who are relegated to the role of participants.

Tombstones

This is a fictional 'tombstone' for a syndicated loan. Megabank UK plc is acting as both arranger and agent, as well as participating in the loan. The participants are shown in alpha numeric order, so the first block of three banks will have committed to provide amounts within one level (perhaps GBP 7,500,000–10,000,000 each) and the second block of nine banks have committed at a lower level (perhaps GBP 2,000,000–5,000,000 each). The tombstone would typically appear in the *Financial Times* and specialist financial magazines, and a perspex block containing the announcement is sent to each of the parties involved.

Attractions of the syndicated loan market

This announcement appears as a matter of record only.

HOME BRIDGING plc

£50,000,000 REVOLVING FACILITY

AGENT

ARBUTHNOT LATHAM
BANK LIMITED

PROVIDED BY

Arbuthnot Latham Bank Limited
Royal Trust Bank (Switzerland)

American Express Bank Ltd
National Australia Bank Limited

Bank of Ireland
The Hongkong and Shanghai Banking Corporation

Yorkshire Bank PLC

AP Bank Limited

Syndicated Lending

This announcement appears as a matter of record only.

A Collins-Wilde Group Company

£25,000,000 SUPPLEMENTAL REVOLVING FACILITY

AGENT

**ARBUTHNOT LATHAM
BANK LIMITED**

PROVIDED BY

Bank of Ireland
Creditanstalt-Bankverein
The Hongkong and Shanghai Banking Corporation

Frankfurt Bukarest Bank AG

Bankco Totta & Açores
NMB Bank, London Branch
Royal Trust Bank (Switzerland)

Al Saudi Banque
Arbuthnot Latham Bank Limited
Crédit Commercial De France
Swiss Cantobank (International)

Syndications timetable – from mandate to drawdown

Phase	Week 1	Week 2	Week 3	Week 4	Week 5	Week 6	Week 7	Week 8
Mandate Awarded	▓							
Prepare first draft of facility agreement with legal counsel	▓	▓						
Prepare information memorandum		▓						
Allocate participations and send invitations to banks		▓						
Review/refine first draft of facility agreement		▓	▓					
Second draft of facility agreement from counsel			▓					
Send Invitations and letters of confidentiality to banks			▓	▓				
Send info memorandum and loan documents to banks			▓	▓				
Wait for banks to obtain individual credit approvals					▓			
Negotiate facility agreement from borrower					▓			
Sign draft facility agreement with borrower					▓			
Wait for banks review facility agreement						▓		
Collect loan administration details						▓	▓	
Make final allocations							▓	
Arrange signing ceremony							▓	
Signing closing								▓
Transfer syndications file to facility agent								▓
Satisfy conditions predecent								▓
DRAWDOWN								▓

Attractions of the syndicated loan market

Exercise 1

Are the following statements true or false?

(A) The arranger and the agent of a syndicated loan must also be participants in the loan.

(B) To regulate the syndicated loans market and ensure a fair chance of success for all borrowers, the Bank of England operates a queuing system under which syndicated loans are allocated a date for the launch of the loan.

(C) As the arranger has structured the syndicated loan, a participant can be assured that if anything were to go wrong in the repayment of the loan, the arranger would repay the participant to protect its own market reputation.

(D) All participants in a syndicated loan receive the same fees.

(E) The borrower can make and receive payments unconnected with the syndicated loan to and from participants.

(F) Once a participant has committed to take part in a syndicated loan, it must retain its participation until the loan is repaid.

(G) The participation of a bank is booked in that bank's principal place of business.

(H) The borrower in a syndicated loan facility must be rated by a rating agency.

Explain the meaning of ...

(I) A 'ring-fenced' loan structure.

(J) 'Scaling back' in the syndication process.

Answers to Exercise 1

(A) False. Although the arranger and the agent will normally also participate in the loan, they do not have to do so, or they may subsequently dispose of their participations through the secondary market. However, if the arranger and the agent do not participate, a potential participant will be likely to question the fundamental creditworthiness of the loan. Arrangers and agents therefore commonly commit to a relatively high level of participation and confirm that they do not intend subsequently to reduce their participation below a certain amount.

(B) False. The Bank of England plays no part in the timing of the launch of a syndicated loan.

(C) False. The loan agreement contains a clause under which each participant declares that it has taken its own independent credit decision, and unless it can prove negligence against the arranger, it cannot rely upon the arranger for repayment.

(D) False. Normally, participants receive two types of fees; a commitment fee and a participation fee. The commitment fee percentage is based upon the undrawn portion of the loan and the percentage rate will be equal for all participants, but the participation fee is staggered according to the percentage of commitment in the loan. The syndicated loan is structured in several bands of commitment, and higher participations attract higher fees.

(E) True. Any participant is entitled to undertake other business with the borrower.

(F) False. A participant may sell all or part of its participation in the secondary market for syndicated loans.

(G) False. In the London market for syndicated loans, many branches of overseas banks book their participations with their London branch. Similarly, a bank may choose to book its participation in an offshore centre for reasons of tax efficiency.

(H) False. Unlike the bond market, it is quite common (especially outside the USA) for borrowers of syndicated loans not to have a formal credit rating. Indeed, borrowers which are not even listed on their local stock exchange have successfully raised syndicated loans.

(I) A 'ring-fenced' structure is one in which assets of the borrower which are received specifically in order to repay a certain syndicated loan are legally separated from other assets of the borrower so that other creditors do not have a claim upon them and the borrower cannot use them in other areas of business.

(J) When a syndicated loan is launched, it is presented as having a specified limit and it is possible that the arranger may receive participation commitments totalling more than this limit. In this case, the borrower has the option of increasing the limit to a higher figure to accommodate all the commitments, or requesting the arranger to 'scale back' the commitments rateably, so that the original facility limit is retained and participants are allocated percentages of the total loan lower than their desired commitments.

Chapter 3

Responsibilities and obligations of syndicated loan participants

As well as gaining the benefits of the syndicated loans market, the parties involved all have definite responsibilities and obligations to which they must adhere. These duties are described in the section on an introduction to syndicated loans of Chapter 1.

The borrower

The information memorandum

The information memorandum is prepared by the arranger in consultation with the borrower and possibly the borrower's accountants and legal advisers. The borrower would trigger an Event of Default under the terms and conditions of the loan agreement – giving the participants the right to call for immediate repayment of the syndicated loan – if it were to make any statement or claim which it knew to be incorrect.

Representations and covenants

The loan agreement is likely to include representations, financial covenants, and restrictions. These will typically include:

If the syndicated loan is unsecured, there will probably be a covenant preventing the borrower from giving security for other loans (i.e. a 'Negative Pledge').

The borrower may not change its main type of business or dispose of significant subsidiaries without the prior written consent of the participants.

There will usually be financial covenants including various ratios concerning net worth, total borrowing, current assets, current liabilities, pre-tax profit, etc. and possibly a restriction on dividends paid to shareholders.

There may well be restrictions on the borrower taking on additional borrowing.

Many syndicated loans are structured as medium-term loans and the borrower must be certain at the time of signing the loan agreement that it will be able to full these covenants at all times without hindering the management of its business and therefore its ability to service the syndicated loan. Any breach of a covenant is viewed seriously and may lead to an increase in the interest margin ('penalty interest') or even an event of default being declared under which the participants may make demand for early repayment of the loan.

Each of the representations and covenants is deemed to be repeated by the borrower each time a loan is 'rolled over' and a new interest period begins.

Events of default

The loan agreement contains a list of events of default, any of which may allow the participants to 'accelerate' the syndicated loan, i.e. call for immediate repayments of all amounts drawn and cancel any undrawn portion. Events of default are typically designed to provide banks with advance warning of potential difficulties (e.g. technical defaults, such as a financial ratio requirement that is violated) to actual difficulties (e.g. financial defaults missing a payment on interest or principle). Other events of default can be defined for matters such as the entry or exit of directors, the acquisition or disposal of subsidiaries or assets, a 'substantial change in the nature of the business', or the contracting of new debt.

How the borrower chooses an arranger for the syndicated loan

A company which is interested in raising a large new syndicated loan is likely to approach more than one bank – or be approached by more than one bank – as potential arranger. Each of these banks will outline their particular strengths and abilities in what is sometimes known as a 'beauty contest' of contestants before the borrower decides which bank to appoint.

In coming to this decision, the borrower will take the following points into consideration:

Placing power

The ability of the potential arranger to attract participants into the syndicated loan. This can best be gauged by studying the recent record of the bank, both from details supplied by the bank and by its position over the last few years in the league tables published in the trade press.

Structuring ability

In certain circumstances, and particularly when the borrower is making an acquisition of another company, it may wish to repay the syndicated loan by issuing bonds or other capital market instruments at some time in the future. A bank which can demonstrate its ability to structure and manage this debt issue can be of enormous benefit to the borrower.

This is one of the reasons why the 1990s witnessed a spate of mergers and acquisitions between banks, such as the creation of the Citibank/ Salornon/Smith Barney/Schroders agglomeration, in which banks with differing specialities have united so that they can offer a borrower a 'one stop' service which can ostensibly handle all the borrower's different needs (if there are no mass defections due to internecine power struggles).

Sector

Some potential arrangers may specialize in particular sectors and concentrate their efforts in these sectors. A thorough understanding of the borrower's sector of business by the arranger is important both to the borrower and to the participants.

Experience

If the arranger is also to act as agent, it should be able to demonstrate an experience and ability to carry out the various functions of the agent throughout the life of the syndicated loan. If it is not to act as agent, it should be able to propose another bank which can satisfactorily perform these functions.

Speed of action

The borrower will wish to be satisfied that the potential arranger can complete the structuring, syndication, documentation and finalization of the syndicated loan within a reasonably short-time scale.

Geographic location

If the borrower is located in a different country or region, it is important that the potential arranger has a thorough understanding of local laws and regulations which may affect the legality and repayment of the loan.

Margins and fees

The pricing of a syndicated loan is a fairly exact science, and it would be unusual for one potential arranger to be drastically out of line with its competitors. However, some banks may be more prepared than others to lower the overall cost to the borrower, particularly by reducing the fees payable.

Underwriting

If the proposed syndicated loan needs to be completed very quickly (and perhaps confidentiality is to be protected by restricting the number of parties having knowledge of the purpose of the proposed loan) the arranger may be asked to assemble a group of underwriters, i.e. a group of banks which will speedily advance the whole amount of the loan by taking very large participations which they will later reduce (usually to a prearranged minimum amount which they will retain in their loan portfolios) when the loan is launched in the syndicated loans market. Because of the size of the commitments which they will initially make, underwriters must have a large balance sheet capacity and be capable of acting quickly and aggressively. The ability of the proposed arranger to assemble a group of underwriters can therefore be vital to the borrower.

The participants and their responsibilities

The responsibilities and obligations of the participant in a syndicated loan are set out in the loan agreement and must be adhered to. They include the following.

Commitment

Once a participant has signed the loan agreement and committed to lend a certain portion of the loan, it must do so even if its own circumstances change. Only if a new law or regulation comes into effect preventing it from contributing may it advise the agent that it can no longer honour its participation.

If one bank is preventing from participating in this way, the other participants must still honour their own commitments unless they are similarly affected by the new law or regulation.

(N.B. In these circumstances the agent will attempt to find a replacement bank and if it is unable to do so within a certain time, the total amount of the syndicated loan will be reduced accordingly. The other participants will not have to raise their own participations to cover the amount lost.)

Event of default

The participant is committed to maintain its participation in the syndicated loan unless an event of default occurs. There may be occasions when a participant feels uneasy about a borrower or the sector or geographic region in which the borrower operates, but it is not possible for the participant to withdraw from the loan or even cancel any undrawn commitment unless a formal event of default has occurred and been announced by the agent.

Majority banks

If an event of default comes to the attention of the agent, it will notify the participants. A meeting of all the participants will normally be held at which the position will be discussed. The participants will then be asked to approve a course of action which may include accelerating the loan. The agent must act in accordance with the instructions of a majority of participants, as defined in the loan agreement and usually consisting of a minimum of 66⅔% in terms of participations ('majority banks'). All participants are then bound to act in accordance with the decision of the majority banks even if they do not agree with this decision.

Similarly, during the course of a syndicated loan the borrower may propose relatively minor amendments to the terms and conditions of the loan, and again the decision on whether or not to agree is made on the basis of the majority banks' views and all participants are bound by this decision. (N.B. This does not apply to the major terms of the syndicated loan, such as the total amount, the repayment schedule, the interest margin and fees, and any security arrangements. Any changes to these items need unanimous approval by all the participants.)

The participants will need to indemnify the agent for any costs and expenses it incurs in carrying out the instructions of the majority banks.

If it is not possible for the participants to reach a 66⅔% majority and therefore a majority bank group view cannot be formed, the agent may

Responsibilities and obligations of syndicated loan participants

act or decide not to act in what it considers to be the best interests of the participants as a whole.

It is often vital for important decisions to be made very quickly, and possibly in a much shorter time frame than is normal for a particular bank's credit process. The bank must be prepared to shortcut its normal processes, probably by reaching a decision and communicating this to the agent and then having the decision subsequently ratified by its credit committee.

Payment sharing

As has already been stated, a participant is free to conduct other business with the borrower during the course of the syndicated loan. However, if a participant wrongly receives a payment from the borrower which should have been paid to the agent and used towards repayment of the syndicated loan, the participant may not retain this amount but must pay it to the agent to be shared amongst all the participants.

Cross default

A participant may make separate credit facilities available to the borrower, or participate in a different syndicated loan to the borrower. If there is any default by the borrower in the conduct of these other facilities, the participant is bound to advise the agent bank of the syndicated loan as this will be an event of default under the provisions of a 'cross default' clause in the loan agreement.

A cross default clause may be limited by giving the borrower a defined period of time to make good this default, and if the position is corrected within this time period an event of default is not deemed to have occurred.

(N.B. Because the borrower has previously signed the loan agreement containing this clause, this notification by the participant to the agent will not be a breach of a bank's normal duty of confidentiality.)

Secondary market sales

A participant is generally free to sell all or part of its participation in the secondary market for syndicated loans. This sale can be made in a number of ways, the most usual of which are by assignment and by novation (the borrower must sign a novation agreement to signify its approval, whereas it does not have to sign or an assignment). However, in doing this the participant must ensure that the bank buying the participation will act in accordance with the same rights and obligations as those which applied to the original participant. To ensure that this is so, most loan agreements now contain a form of transfer by novation which must be used and lodged with the agent.

Other considerations affecting participants in a syndicated loan

Reference banks and interest margins

The rate of interest applied to a syndicated loan is usually expressed in the loan agreement as a percentage above the London Inter Bank Offered Rate ('LIBOR'). In some syndicated loans this rate is periodically determined by a small number of 'reference banks' (which are usually participants in the loan) quoting what they believe to be LIBOR at a stated time and date. The average of these rates will be used to determine the applicable rate for the next interest period of the syndicated loan. However, not all banks are offered funding in the inter bank market at the same rates, and some banks will lose part of the loan margin because their funding costs are relatively high compared with those of the reference banks.

The system of using reference banks has generally been superseded by the use of 'screen rates' defined in the loan agreement, but the possibility of a funding differential still exists.

Payment risk

All payments made in a syndicated loan are routed through the agent. participants should therefore recognize that there is a payment risk on the agent.

The agent's role in a default situation

In the event of there being difficulties during the course of the syndicated loan, or an event of default occurring, the agent's role in advising the participants, negotiating with the borrower and taking any remedial action decided upon, is crucial. Therefore potential participants must be confident that the agent is capable of carrying out these functions to the satisfaction of the participants.

Roles of the arranger and the agent

The arranger and the agent are key figures in a syndicated loan.

The arranger arranges the loan and the underlying structure, is responsible for the information memorandum, deals with the syndication, appoints solicitors to draw up the loan documentation and give legal opinions on the validity of the loan, and arranges for the loan agreement to be signed by all parties to it.

The agent arranges for disbursement to be made, keeps records on behalf of the participants of all payments made and received and any changes in participations made through the secondary market, distributes financial information to the participants during the life of the loan, oversees repayments, and in the event of a default it provides a lead to the participants as to which options are available and advisable, and then takes whatever actions are necessary to carry out the instructions of the participants. (In most of these functions it is possible for the agent to share these tasks with other banks, or appoint other banks to take over responsibility for specific tasks, if the workload involved would otherwise be too cumbersome for the proper functioning of the syndicated loan.) These are the major responsibilities of the agent, and are dealt with in more detail elsewhere in this book, but in addition the agent has other obligations as follows:

Sharing information

The agent is obliged to pass on to the participants any information it receives, especially any which could lead to a default under the terms and conditions of the loan agreement.

Conditions Precedent

The loan agreement is likely to contain a series of conditions which must be met before the syndicated loan may be disbursed. These are known as Conditions Precedent and will typically include items such as:

- *Legal opinions*: these are given by the solicitors acting on behalf of the syndicate and confirm the legal validity of the loan. If the borrower is domiciled abroad, or part of the loan is dependent upon operations in a foreign country, there will also be another legal opinion from solicitors in that country stating that no local laws or regulations are breached by the terms and conditions of the syndicated loan. At the time that the loan agreement is signed, these opinions are given in a conditional form, stating that if the loan agreement is signed in this form, it will be valid and enforceable. Once the loan agreement has been signed, the actual opinions are forwarded to the agent.
- *Security*: if security is given as a condition of the syndicated loan, the security arrangements may not be perfected at the time of signing the loan agreement.
- *Notice of Drawdown*: the borrower will be required to submit to the agent a Notice of Drawdown, in a form detailed in the loan agreement, requesting disbursement of the syndicated loan.

One of the agent's key responsibilities is to ensure that all Conditions Precedent have been fulfilled, and to notify the participants accordingly, before the loan is disbursed in accordance with the notice of drawdown.

Documentation

It is the responsibility of the arranger to appoint solicitors to act on behalf of the participants to prepare the loan documentation and ancillary documentation such as guarantees. The borrower will appoint its own solicitors to represent its interests and agree the documentation on the borrower's behalf. This process involves a close cooperation between the syndicate's solicitors and the arranger, and attention to detail in ensuring that all points are accurately worded and all contingencies covered, as the loan documentation is designed to meet every eventuality and to determine all future courses of action. Once the documentation is prepared, it is sent to all the participants for their comments and amended if necessary.

A signing ceremony is usually arranged at which the loan agreement is signed in sufficient numbers that each party retains an original signed copy. If required, each party is subsequently provided with additional conformed copies of the original.

Other appointments

Depending upon the structure of the syndicated loan, it may be necessary for the agent to appoint other institutions to specified roles such as security trustees or independent technical advisers to the participants. These positions are dealt with in the Project Finance Book in this series.

Exercise 2

Are the following statements true or false?

(A) The borrower consults with its accountants and legal advisers when it prepares the information memorandum.

(B) A negative pledge is an undertaking given by the borrower that it will not take on additional borrowing while the syndicated loan remains outstanding.

(C) The 'acceleration' of a syndicated loan means that the borrower chooses to repay it ahead of schedule.

(D) The geographic location of the arranger and the agent is not important.

(E) An underwriter participates in a loan on a 'take and hold' basis.

(F) If a bank commits to take a participation in a syndicated loan but is then acquired by another bank before the loan is disbursed, the new owner can withdraw from this commitment under the Conditions Precedent clause in the loan agreement. Why?

(G) Why would an agent bank act against its own judgement?

(H) Why would an agent state that a syndicated loan is incapable of being drawn?

(I) Why would a bank ignore its duty of confidentiality to a customer?

(J) Why should the finance director of a potential borrower spend his time at a beauty contest?

Answers to Exercise 2

(A) False. The borrower does not prepare the information memorandum? this is done by the arranger in consultation with the borrower.

(B) False. A negative pledge is an undertaking given by the borrower that it will not give security for any other borrowings without receiving the prior written consent of the participants.

(C) False. 'acceleration' is a term used to signify an early demand for immediate repayment of a syndicated loan following an event of default made by the borrower.

(D) True. The arranger and the agent may be based in a different country to the borrower; however it is very important that they are both aware of all local laws and regulations which may impact upon the syndicated loan.

(E) Usually true. An underwriter will take a large initial participation in a loan on the basis that it will subsequently reduce this participation down to a minimum amount which it will hold.

(F) False. The bank remains committed. The Conditions Precedent clause relates to actions which must be fulfilled by the borrower before disbursement of the syndicated loan may be made.

(G) An agent is obliged to act in accordance with decisions made by a majority bank group following an event of default, even though the agent may disagree with the course of action decided upon.

(H) An agent has to declare that all Conditions Precedent have been fulfilled before the loan may be disbursed. If it is unable to do so before the expiration of the commitment period, the loan is cancelled.

(I) By signing the loan agreement, the borrower agrees to all its terms and conditions, including the actions which participant banks may take in defined circumstances. One of these relates to the cross default clause, where a bank must notify the agent if the borrower defaults in another loan facility it has taken from the participant.

(J) A beauty contest is the term used to describe a situation in which several potential arrangers will make presentations to a company intending to raise a syndicated loan, explaining why they believe they are best placed to act as arranger for the loan.

Chapter 4

The major players in the syndicated loans market

We now consider the details of the major players in the syndicated loans market, and their relative positions in annual league tables. We will also consider various examples of structures used in syndicated loans and the various ways in which the arranger and the borrower may agree the loan is to be repaid. This includes the details of a major recently finalized syndicated loan, with detailed analysis of the structure of the loan and how this was viewed by potential participants in making their credit decisions.

League tables are used to analyse the growth of the syndicated loans market as well as the performance of banks which participate in it. They are also useful to measure the relative performances of different banks in terms of the total value of loans which they arrange in a year, and in various geographic or industry sector categories.

In this chapter, we will show some of these league tables to demonstrate the major players in the syndicated loans market in the year 2003, both banks and borrowers.

League tables

For banks, there are many different types of league tables. Some show the ratings of banks in any role in a syndication, some for specialized positions such as arranger or book runner.

Syndicated Lending

Some list the largest borrowers by category, or largest banks in specific geographic zones.

Here, we provide various league tables for different areas and industry sectors.

This data is compiled by London-based Dealogic plc (ex Capital-Data). Dealogic keeps track not only of syndicated lending activity but also the specific subset of syndicated lending known as project finance.

Mandated arranger rankings for global syndicated loans

Mandated arranger rankings for global syndicated loans:
01 January 2003–31 December 2003

Pos.	Bank name	Amount USD (mn)	No.	Share (%)
1	Citigroup Inc	198,227	742	10.49
2	JP Morgan	193,678	824	10.24
3	Bank of America Corp	164,455	1048	8.70
4	Deutsche Bank AG	82,513	355	4.36
5	Barclays	80,827	328	4.28
6	Bank One	68,080	540	3.60
7	BNP Paribas	66,660	360	3.53
8	ABN AMRO	60,386	437	3.19
9	HSBC	59,810	284	3.16
10	Wachovia Corp	52,642	587	2.78
11	Royal Bank of Scotland	47,655	244	2.52
12	Mizuho	45,580	281	2.41
13	Credit Agricole – Credit Lyonnais	42,894	259	2.27
14	FleetBoston	40,474	449	2.14
15	Mitsubishi Tokyo Financial Group Inc	38,699	325	2.05
16	Credit Suisse First Boston	37,550	166	1.99
17	Sumitomo Mitsui Banking Corp	35,645	363	1.89
18	Dresdner Kleinwort Wasserstein	32,293	91	1.71
19	SG	30,156	178	1.60
20	UBS	17,927	97	0.95

Source: Dealogic, 2003

This table lists the largest arrangers of syndicated loans worldwide. Readers will undoubtedly notice that the top tiers of banks are US banks. Part of the reason for this is that around 50% of syndicated lending volume is in the USA, and it is only natural that US banks be ranked according to the volume of syndicated loans underwritten in the USA. There are however other players as we will see in subsequent league tables.

Mandated arranger rankings for US syndicated loans

Mandated arranger rankings for US syndicated loans:
01 January 2003–31 December 2003

Pos.	Bank name	Amount USD (mn)	No.	Share (%)
1	Bank of America Corp	155,646	1006	15.61
2	JP Morgan	150,356	709	15.08
3	Citigroup Inc	124,955	484	12.53
4	Bank One	66,132	532	6.63
5	Wachovia Corp	52,370	573	5.25
6	Deutsche Bank AG	46,203	219	4.63
7	FleetBoston	40,225	444	4.03
8	ABN AMRO	28,498	256	2.86
9	Credit Suisse First Boston	28,206	141	2.83
10	Barclays	24,999	102	2.51
11	BNP Paribas	24,433	140	2.45
12	GE Capital Group	15,477	178	1.55
13	Scotia Capital	14,236	114	1.43
14	Wells Fargo Bank NA	13,252	165	1.33
15	Bank of New York	13,095	112	1.31
16	SunTrust Banks Inc	13,042	165	1.31
17	UBS	12,669	83	1.27
18	Morgan Stanley	11,881	39	1.19
19	Mitsubishi Tokyo Financial Group Inc	10,827	107	1.09
20	Lehman Brothers	10,362	85	1.04

Source: Dealogic, 2003

As we would expect, the list for North American borrowers is dominated by North American banks, but there are some creditable performances by European banks.

Mandated arranger rankings for EMEA syndicated loans

Mandated arranger rankings for EMEA syndicated loans:
01 January 2003–31 December 2003

Pos.	Bank name	Amount USD (mn)	No.	Share (%)
1	Citigroup Inc	54,910	159	8.32
2	Barclays	52,017	197	7.88
3	HSBC	44,587	148	6.76
4	Royal Bank of Scotland	40,334	183	6.11
5	BNP Paribas	38,757	167	5.87
6	JP Morgan	37,914	88	5.74
7	Deutsche Bank AG	33,824	112	5.12
8	Credit Agricole – Credit Lyonnais	31,299	128	4.74
9	Dresdner Kleinwort Wasserstein	29,711	81	4.50
10	ABN AMRO	27,170	123	4.12
11	SG	23,226	104	3.52
12	ING	14,651	107	2.22
13	WestLB AG	12,150	73	1.84
14	Commerzbank AG	10,777	61	1.63
15	Bank of Scotland	9331	49	1.41
16	Nordea AB	8676	55	1.31
17	Credit Suisse First Boston	8205	20	1.24
18	Lloyds TSB Capital Markets	7961	50	1.21
19	UniCredit Banca Mobiliare	7676	17	1.16
20	Banco Bilbao Vizcaya Argentaria SA – BBVA	7443	59	1.13

Source: Dealogic, 2003

For loans in other countries the North American banks are less well represented, in the EMEA region, this is only natural as the UK banks leverage on their network of international and commonwealth contacts, and the main internationally oriented German and Dutch banks underwrite business for their clients in the London markets. These well-oiled syndication teams can naturally compete on price and reach with the other major international competitors.

Mandated arranger rankings for Asia-Pacific syndicated loans

Mandated arranger rankings for Asia-Pacific syndicated loans:
01 January 2003–31 December 2003

Pos.	Bank name	Amount USD (mn)	No.	Share (%)
1	Mizuho	38,922	230	19.46
2	Sumitomo Mitsui Banking Corp	31,084	314	15.54
3	Mitsubishi Tokyo Financial Group Inc	23,332	157	11.67
4	Citigroup Inc	14,240	84	7.12
5	HSBC	7509	89	3.75
6	Australia & New Zealand Banking Group Ltd	5262	54	2.63
7	Westpac Banking Corp	4989	40	2.49
8	National Australia Bank Ltd	4897	36	2.45
9	Standard Chartered Bank	4105	79	2.05
10	ABN AMRO	3898	50	1.95
11	Credit Agricole – Credit Lyonnais	3200	54	1.60
12	Bank of China	3134	40	1.57
13	Industrial & Commercial Bank of China	3070	27	1.53
14	Commonwealth Bank of Australia	3017	38	1.51
15	BNP Paribas	2866	43	1.43
16	UFJ Group	2402	28	1.20
17	DBS Bank Ltd	2370	50	1.19
18	Deutsche Bank AG	2345	11	1.17
19	JP Morgan	2301	15	1.15
20	Barclays	2208	23	1.10

Source: Dealogic, 2003

The Asian syndicated lending market not surprisingly are led by the Japanese leviathans with large balance sheet availability and strong underwriting relationships with Japanese banks as well as close links to Japanese industrial groupings. There are however other geographic regions in Asia including China and Australia which affect the league tables, and of course, the US banks acting in the context of Japanese–US trade.

Top 20 providers for global syndicated loans in 2003

Top 20 providers for global syndicated loans in 2003

Pos.	Bank name	Amount USD (mn)	No.	Share (%)
1	JP Morgan	105,598	1107	5.56
2	Citigroup Inc	86,654	1011	4.56
3	Bank of America Corp	78,644	1343	4.14
4	Deutsche Bank AG	55,026	647	2.90
5	ABN AMRO	52,096	965	2.74
6	Barclays plc	50,326	629	2.65
7	BNP Paribas	50,149	824	2.64
8	Bank One	48,145	864	2.53
9	Mitsubishi Tokyo Financial Group Inc	46,920	990	2.47
10	HSBC	46,824	678	2.46
11	Credit Agricole – Credit Lyonnais	46,160	713	2.43
12	Wachovia Corp	46,083	928	2.43
13	Royal Bank of Scotland	43,559	586	2.29
14	Credit Suisse First Boston	40,202	446	2.12
15	Mizuho	36,189	712	1.90
16	FleetBoston	33,963	779	1.79
17	SG	31,582	497	1.66
18	Sumitomo Mitsui Banking Corp	30,237	726	1.59
19	ING	27,234	538	1.43
20	Scotia Capital	24,844	500	1.31

Volumes based on equal apportionment when allocations are undisclosed.
Source: Dealogic, 2003

Providers advance funds as opposed to underwriting them. In this league table of worldwide providers of syndicated loans, the US banks figure prominently due to their large sizes following the wave of mergers witnessed in the 1990s and balance sheet availability. The Japanese banks are suffering from asset quality problems and capitalization ratio constraints with the result that their rankings are somewhat lower.

It is important to note that the development of the secondary asset markets and increased homogenization of syndicated loans, as evidenced by standardized loan documentation sponsored by the Loan Marketing

Association in the UK and Loan Syndications Trading Association in the USA, coupled with the penetration of the rating agencies in the syndicated loan Markets (a new development from their traditional role in the equity markets which we cover in Chapter 8) mean that the providers can later offload these loan participations on the secondary markets more easily than say 10 or 15 years ago.

Top 20 providers for US syndicated loans in 2003

Top 20 providers for US syndicated loans in 2003

Pos.	Bank name	Amount USD (mn)	No.	Share (%)
1	JP Morgan	82,657	921	8.21
2	Bank of America Corp	71,065	1240	7.06
3	Citigroup Inc	54,045	635	5.37
4	Bank One	44,845	813	4.46
5	Wachovia Corp	44,194	858	4.39
6	Deutsche Bank AG	35,010	391	3.48
7	FleetBoston	32,322	740	3.21
8	Credit Suisse First Boston	31,379	349	3.12
9	ABN AMRO	30,488	630	3.03
10	BNP Paribas	23,206	382	2.31
11	Mitsubishi Tokyo Financial Group Inc	18,880	471	1.88
12	Wells Fargo Bank NA	18,615	531	1.85
13	Scotia Capital	18,600	363	1.85
14	Bank of New York	18,334	417	1.82
15	SunTrust Banks Inc	17,288	403	1.72
16	Barclays plc	16,177	249	1.61
17	US Bancorp	15,343	471	1.52
18	UBS	15,262	244	1.52
19	Merrill Lynch & Co Inc	14,762	280	1.47
20	Morgan Stanley	14,741	201	1.46

Volumes based on equal apportionment when allocations are undisclosed.
Source: Dealogic, 2003

Not surprisingly, the major providers of funds in the US markets are the large US banks, however, it should be noted that much of these retained amounts are subsequently traded in secondary asset markets.

Top 20 providers for EMEA syndicated loans in 2003

Top 20 providers for EMEA syndicated loans in 2003

Pos.	Bank name	Amount USD (mn)	No.	Share (%)
1	Barclays plc	31,712	343	4.80
2	Royal Bank of Scotland	31,382	353	4.75
3	Credit Agricole – Credit Lyonnais	29,127	337	4.41
4	HSBC	27,607	306	4.18
5	Citigroup Inc	24,165	249	3.66
6	BNP Paribas	21,960	317	3.32
7	JP Morgan	19,918	143	3.02
8	ABN AMRO	18,479	246	2.80
9	SG	18,451	248	2.79
10	ING	18,269	311	2.77
11	Deutsche Bank AG	17,674	210	2.68
12	WestLB AG	13,415	188	2.03
13	Bank of Scotland	12,122	150	1.84
14	Dresdner Kleinwort Wasserstein	11,424	180	1.73
15	Commerzbank AG	11,357	263	1.72
16	Lloyds TSB Capital Markets	10,633	199	1.61
17	HVB Group	10,564	233	1.60
18	Fortis	10,498	211	1.59
19	Banco Bilbao Vizcaya Argentaria SA – BBVA	9807	156	1.48
20	BayernLB	9802	199	1.48

Volumes based on equal apportionment when allocations are undisclosed.
Source: Dealogic, 2003

As in Table 4.1.6, the league tables for major providers of funds in the EMEA markets not surprisingly include many European banks, although there are also some US banks. Given the prominence of US banks as underwriters in the EMEA region in Table 4.1.3, this suggests that the US banks are more active as underwriters than in classic take and hold lending (e.g. they originate the deals but either fully syndicate them or offload them on the secondary markets, thereby earning transaction fees and maintaining unencumbered balance sheets for future lending opportunities.

Top 20 providers for Asia-Pacific syndicated loans in 2003

Top 20 providers for Asia-Pacific syndicated loans in 2003

Pos.	Bank name	Amount USD (mn)	No.	Share (%)
1	Mizuho	21,542	422	11.05
2	Mitsubishi Tokyo Financial Group Inc	19,666	346	10.09
3	Sumitomo Mitsui Banking Corp	17,204	454	8.83
4	Citigroup Inc	6979	93	3.58
5	UFJ Group	6085	229	3.12
6	HSBC	5913	136	3.03
7	Sumitomo Trust & Banking Co	5356	103	2.75
8	Australia & New Zealand Banking Group Ltd	5352	80	2.75
9	Norinchukin Bank	4790	101	2.46
10	Westpac Banking Corp	4332	59	2.22
11	National Australia Bank Ltd	3844	63	1.97
12	Resona Holdings Co Ltd	3798	126	1.95
13	Bank of China	3522	83	1.81
14	Commonwealth Bank of Australia	3423	60	1.76
15	BNP Paribas	3407	84	1.75
16	Credit Agricole – Credit Lyonnais	2714	87	1.39
17	Industrial & Commercial Bank of China	2700	85	1.39
18	ABN AMRO	2364	63	1.21
19	Standard Chartered Bank	2350	86	1.21
20	China Development Bank	2275	4	1.17

Volumes based on equal apportionment when allocations are undisclosed.
Source: Dealogic, 2003

As in Table 4.1.7, we see a similar development with the proviso that the major providers in this case are Japanese rather than European banks.

Top 20 global borrowers of syndicated loans in 2003

Top 20 borrowers globally of syndicated loans in 2003

Pos.	borrower name	Amount USD (mn)	No.	Share (%)
1	Network Rail Ltd	15,091	1	0.79
2	General Electric Capital Corp	13,620	1	0.71
3	DaimlerChrysler AG	13,000	1	0.68
4	Volkswagen AG	11,346	1	0.59
5	Vodafone plc	10,400	1	0.54
6	Olivetti SpA	9876	1	0.51
7	Alstom SA	9203	6	0.48
8	E.ON AG	9154	1	0.48
9	Autostrade per l'Italia SpA	8945	1	0.47
10	Bayerische Motoren Werke AG – BMW	8500	2	0.44
11	General Motors Acceptance Corp (GMAC)	8500	1	0.44
12	Morgan Stanley & Co	7882	2	0.41
13	Allied Waste Industries Inc	7500	3	0.39
14	Quincy Capital Corp	7446	8	0.39
15	Suez	7342	2	0.38
16	Telecom Italia SpA	7133	1	0.37
17	Time Warner Cable Inc	7100	3	0.37
18	Vivendi Universal SA	7060	3	0.37
19	Sears Roebuck Acceptance Corp	7000	2	0.36
20	UNEDIC	6937	3	0.36

Source: Dealogic, 2003

Here we see the major borrowers ranked internationally, and it is evident that they are typically large infrastructure development entities or manufacturing entities either renegotiating existing credit facilities or investing in capital goods or cross border expansion. Many of these borrowers are also driven by acquisition sprees.

Top 20 US borrowers of syndicated loans in 2003

Top 20 US borrowers of syndicated loans in 2003

Pos.	borrower name	Amount USD (mn)	No.	Share (%)
1	General Electric Capital Corp	13,620	1	1.39
2	General Motors Acceptance Corp (GMAC)	8500	1	0.87
3	Morgan Stanley & Co	7882	2	0.80
4	Allied Waste Industries Inc	7500	3	0.76
5	Quincy Capital Corp	7446	8	0.76
6	Time Warner Cable Inc	7100	3	0.72
7	Sears Roebuck Acceptance Corp	7000	2	0.71
8	General Motors Corp	6426	2	0.66
9	CenterPoint Energy Inc	6400	3	0.65
10	Reliant Resources inc.	6233	1	0.64
11	Dean Foods Co	5500	2	0.56
12	American Express Co	5350	1	0.55
13	Charter Communications Operating LLC	5167	1	0.53
14	TRW Automotive Inc	5003	3	0.51
15	Verizon Communications Inc	5000	1	0.51
16	International Lease Finance Corp	4900	2	0.50
17	Citigroup Global Markets Holdings Inc	4825	1	0.49
18	Exxon Mobil Corp	4806	1	0.49
19	Enterprise Funding Corp	4784	7	0.49
20	Boeing Co	4731	2	0.48

Source: Dealogic, 2003

Top 20 EMEA borrowers of syndicated loans in 2003

Top 20 EMEA borrowers of syndicated loans in 2003

Pos.	borrower name	Amount USD (mn)	No.	Share (%)
1	Network Rail Ltd	15,091	1	2.29
2	DaimlerChrysler AG	13,000	1	1.97
3	Volkswagen AG	11,346	1	1.72
4	Vodafone plc	10400	1	1.58
5	Olivetti SpA	9876	1	1.50
6	Alstom SA	9203	6	1.40
7	E.ON AG	9154	1	1.39
8	Autostrade per l'Italia SpA	8945	1	1.36
9	Bayerische Motoren Werke AG – BMW	8500	2	1.29
10	Suez	7342	2	1.11
11	Telecom Italia SpA	7133	1	1.08
12	Vivendi Universal SA	7060	3	1.07
13	UNEDIC	6937	3	1.05
14	Clearstream International	6850	1	1.04
15	Gas Natural SDG SA	6819	1	1.03
16	Electricite de France SA (EDF)	6414	1	0.97
17	Schweizerische Rueckversicherungs–Gesellschaft–Swiss Re	6000	1	0.91
18	Deutsche Telekom AG	5710	1	0.87
19	Energie Baden Wurttemberg AG – EnBW	5643	2	0.86
20	Capital Management & Investment plc	5506	1	0.83

Source: Dealogic, 2003

Tables 4.1.10 and 4.1.11 offer a typical breakdown of each zone's major industrial and infrastructural groupings. It should be noted that a substantial portion of these loans are destined to take out and refinance existing credit agreements and do not necessarily represent borrowings for 'new money needs'.

Top 20 Asia-Pacific borrowers of syndicated loans in 2003

Top 20 Asia-Pacific borrowers of syndicated loans in 2003

Pos.	borrower name	Amount USD (mn)	No.	Share (%)
1	Mitsubishi Corp	4805	2	2.44
2	Itochu Corp	4082	3	2.07
3	Marubeni Corp	3580	3	1.82
4	Toshiba Corp	3195	5	1.62
5	Nissan Motor Co Ltd	3116	2	1.58
6	Recruit Co Ltd	3092	3	1.57
7	Yunnan Huaneng Lancangjiang Hydropower Co (Xiaowan Power Station)	3020	1	1.53
8	Orient Corp (ORICO)	2934	1	1.49
9	Mitsubishi Motors Corp (MMC)	2888	3	1.47
10	CNOOC & Shell Petrochemicals Co Ltd	2677	1	1.36
11	Fujitsu Ltd	2336	2	1.19
12	Burns Philip & Co Ltd	2193	2	1.11
13	Japan Telecom Co Ltd	2038	1	1.03
14	NEC Corp	2030	2	1.03
15	AMP Group Finance Services	1988	1	1.01
16	Alinta Networks Holdings Pty Ltd	1784	3	0.91
17	Sumitomo Corp	1781	2	0.90
18	Abbott Japan Co Ltd	1776	2	0.90
19	Mazda Motor Corp	1671	3	0.85
20	Tokyo Electric Power Co Inc	1664	1	0.84

Source: Dealogic, 2003

Industry volume table for global syndicated loans in 2003

Industry volume table for global syndicated loans in 2003

	Total amount USD (mn)	No.
Finance	283,892	596
Utility and power	178,139	361
Telecommunications	148,113	229
Oil and gas	121,299	348
Retail	93,053	269
Transportation	91,488	285
Real estate	88,030	418
Automobile	86,962	136
Construction/building	71,699	308
Food and beverage	69,765	214
Healthcare	68,950	242
Insurance	66,046	110
Computers	62,558	287
Consumer products	58,349	193
Services	51,027	206
Leisure and recreation	44,663	110
Metal and steel	43,346	148
Chemicals	42,130	161
Publishing	37,589	72
Dining and lodging	32,949	76
Forestry and paper	29,489	79
Holding companies	27,415	55
Government	19,813	54
Machinery	19,569	103
Mining	18,781	68
Aerospace/aircraft	16,668	20
Defence and aerospace	16,285	19
Other	13,340	29
Textile	10,521	84
Agribusiness	6142	29
Unclassified	561	5
Total	191,863,1	5311

Source: Dealogic, 2003

The major players in the syndicated loans market

This table is interesting in that it confirms that the main industry sectors for borrowing are the financial sector (typically refinancing existing debts into more advantageous structures) and the 'big 4' of infrastructure categories (power, telecommunications, oil and gas, and transportation). The next major sectors are domestic consumer driven – retail trades and construction activity.

Industry volume table for US syndicated loans in 2003

Industry volume table for US syndicated loans in 2003

	Total amount USD (mn)	No.
Finance	168,074	247
Utility and power	82,862	184
Oil and gas	73,783	216
Telecommunications	65,376	104
Retail	53,987	154
Healthcare	51,649	190
Real estate	44,768	252
Food and beverage	43,159	111
Insurance	42,061	75
Consumer products	38,372	111
Computers	34,126	114
Automobile	30,289	68
Leisure and recreation	29,951	75
Services	24,942	139
Construction/building	23,839	142
Transportation	23,666	83
Chemicals	19,605	65
Metal and steel	16,927	67
Dining and lodging	16,226	45
Machinery	15,199	50
Publishing	14,542	34
Forestry and paper	13,930	37
Defence and aerospace	11,000	13
Holding companies	9205	19
Textile	7677	47
Aerospace/aircraft	6848	10
Government	5535	10
Other	4842	14
Mining	4841	21
Agribusiness	3159	15
Unclassified	320	2
Total	980,757	2712

Source: Dealogic, 2003

Industry volume table for EMEA syndicated loans in 2003

Industry volume table for EMEA syndicated loans in 2003

	Total amount USD (mn)	No.
Finance	77,660	208
Utility and power	72,070	102
Telecommunications	68,602	60
Transportation	49,086	93
Automobile	45,740	30
Construction/building	38,537	77
Retail	31,436	53
Real estate	30,859	97
Oil and gas	29,084	69
Services	20,993	36
Publishing	19,050	24
Food and beverage	17,174	44
Dining and lodging	16,122	21
Insurance	15,637	19
Chemicals	14,356	38
Metal and steel	14,223	31
Healthcare	13,710	29
Leisure and recreation	12,483	18
Consumer products	11,177	37
Forestry and paper	10,059	19
Mining	8516	19
Other	8288	9
Holding companies	7580	19
Computers	7224	29
Government	6256	27
Defence and aerospace	5236	5
Aerospace/aircraft	3651	4
Machinery	1873	11
Textile	1443	14
Agribusiness	1350	7
Unclassified	223	2
Total	659,699	1251

Source: Dealogic, 2003

Industry volume table for Asia-Pacific syndicated loans in 2003

Industry volume table for Asia-Pacific syndicated loans in 2003

	Total amount USD (mn)	No.
Finance	26,733	121
Computers	19,636	139
Utility and power	17,654	54
Transportation	14,478	94
Real estate	12,208	67
Telecommunications	11,297	48
Holding companies	9575	12
Automobile	9274	32
Construction/building	8553	86
Consumer products	8144	40
Oil and gas	6851	36
Chemicals	6263	46
Metal and steel	5833	35
Food and beverage	5658	43
Retail	5579	52
Services	4792	29
Forestry and paper	4103	18
Healthcare	3591	23
Mining	2671	19
Machinery	2423	41
Government	2264	9
Leisure and recreation	2154	16
Insurance	1988	1
Agribusiness	1633	7
Publishing	1473	9
Textile	1360	22
Dining and lodging	525	9
Other	200	5
Defence and aerospace	49	1
Unclassified	18	1
Aerospace/aircraft	0	0
Total	196,980	1114

Source: Dealogic, 2003

Tables 4.1.14, 4.1.15, and 4.1.16 are all broadly similar with the observations made in Table 4.1.13 with the exception that Computers figure prominently in Asia-Pacific, no doubt driven by the fact that this geographic zone is the major manufacturing centre for IT equipment. Despite the fact that much computer equipment features the logos of well known Western companies; the reality is that the components are manufactured to specifications by Asian manufacturers, whom require considerable investment in plant and infrastructure. Such league tables are useful as a gauge of economic activity in the region.

Barclays Capital

Barclays Capital is one of the leading British banks in the syndicated loans market, and in most league tables it is the top tier of European banks. Deutsche Bank is its most serious European competitor, with ABN AMRO not far behind.

For example, amongst European banks arranging pan-European deals during the year 2003, Barclays Capital had a 7.8% market share, HSBC 6.7%, and RBS 6.1% (Table 4.1.3).

Here, we will give a brief profile of Barclays Capital to illustrate how a leading bank in the syndicated loans market may be structured, and the strategic priorities they may have.

Barclays Capital is the investment banking division of the Barclays Bank group. It is based in London, from where it covers the UK, continental Europe, the Middle East and Africa. It also has offices in New York (for North American Business), Miami (for South America), Tokyo and Hong Kong (for South East Asia) and Sydney (for Australasia). All the overseas offices report to the global head of syndications and loan distribution in London. Its activities include arranging and underwriting primary loan syndications for target clients, executing individual and bulk loan sales to facilitate the management of the Barclays Group's loan portfolio, loan trading and sales.

Barclays Capital covers the syndicated loans market and the bonds market. The two divisions exist side by side – some banks have merged these divisions to offer a 'one stop' solution to the increasing number of borrowers who wish to repay a syndicated loan by means of a bond issue. Barclays Capital have not taken this step because of the different business cultures and characteristics of the two activities.

Because of the worldwide spread of branches of Barclays Bank, virtually all syndicated loans arranged by Barclays Capital are made to existing customers. They are unlikely actively to seek mandates from companies which are not existing customers, although they may be invited to join a loan as joint arranger or book runner (i.e. agent) to a non-customer. They consider it strategically vital to have other business relationships with the borrower so that overall profitability is maximized. There are internal guidelines on returns and profitability which must be achieved.

A cross-section of names they have arranged for Euroloans in the late 1990s includes:

- Adam Opel GmbH (Euro 650 mn)/General Motors (USD 3 bn)
- Al–Taweelah A2-Emirates CMS Power Co. (USD 596 mn)
- Banque PSA Finance (EUR 1.85 bn)
- BMW AG (GBP 3 bn)
- Framatone S.A. (USD 400 mn)
- Kappa Packaging (NLG 1.7 bn)
- National Grid Group (USD 3.15 bn)
- Turkiye Garanti Bankasi (USD 250 mn)
- Vodafone AirTouch plc (USD 10.5 bn)
- Wolverhampton & Dudley Breweries (GBP 350 mn)

The international spread of business can be seen from the above. Whereas some years ago loan syndication business was weighted in favour of UK mandates to the extent of 65:35%, the majority now come from outside the UK.

Opportunities to arrange a syndicated loan are normally brought to the attention of Barclays Capital by the relationship manager for the company concerned. A team is then formed, consisting of a senior manager from each of the origination, distribution, loan transaction management, and perhaps legal divisions, plus the relationship manager, to examine the borrower's requirements and to discuss alternative solutions. If appropriate, the team will also include a senior manager from the bond division. Once a strategy has been agreed by the team, a presentation with a term sheet is made to the company and, hopefully, a detailed mandate letter will be signed. Each senior manager will expect to be working on a minimum of 15 transactions at any one time.

Although Barclays Capital does not concentrate on any particular business sector, it has built up particular strengths in sectors such as merger and acquisition finance, telecom, property, project finance, oil and gas, and utilities.

Another recent development in the syndicated loans market with which Barclays Capital has been involved is the underwriting of the whole amount of a loan which is then placed straight into the secondary market, rather than first going into general syndication in the traditional way. This has encouraged the growth of the secondary market, which Barclays Capital has encouraged since it became one of the founder members of the Loan Market Association in 1996. Both these topics are examined in greater detail in Chapter 8.

Chapter 5

Structures used in syndicated loans

As noted previously, a syndicated loan is a loan which is provided by two or more banks. Any loan can be syndicated, be it large or small, simple or complex. But in the London Syndicated Loans Market, the way that loans are structured will normally comply with certain general characteristics.

Overview of syndications

There are three types of syndications.

Underwritten transactions

These are also known as a 'Bought Deal', under which the whole amount of the facility is guaranteed to the borrower with all the terms and conditions agreed in advance. The loan is underwritten by an arranger who takes the entire transaction risk and will be responsible for the syndication process. Underwritten transactions are often found in situations where a short turnaround period is required, such as acquisition finance, and sufficient time would not be available for the normal syndication process. The attraction to the borrower is the speed at which the deal can be finalized and the protection of confidential and price-sensitive information, but the borrower will expect to pay higher than normal fees to the arranger. If the size of the loan is very high, there may be two or three joint arrangers.

Arranged or best efforts transactions

Here, the arranger provides a commitment for the amount it will lend and agrees to arrange and syndicate the balance of the loan on a 'best efforts' basis, i.e. it does not guarantee that the whole required amount can be raised. This type of transaction is suited to a borrower which is confident that the full amount of the loan will be raised, and would appreciate some new banking relationships. The borrower is taking the market risk and has no certainty that the full amount can be raised, but will be paying a smaller fee to the arranger.

Club deals

These are transactions under which the borrower self-syndicates the loan to the market, using its existing relationship banks. The borrower effectively becomes the arranger and the agent, and the participating banks have to have a strong enough relationship with the borrower to part-finance a project without the joint strength that a syndicated loan can bring. Different situations bring about different structures, but there will be identical documentation with the different banks.

Term of loan

Generally, loans of 1 or 2 years' duration are known as short term, up to 5 years as medium term, and over 5 years as long term.

Most banks prefer to limit their lending to loans with a repayment period of up to 5 years. There are always exceptions, such as aircraft financings or some project financings, but these tend to be somewhat specialized and concentrated amongst banks with a strong degree of experience and expertise in those sectors. The perceived risk in a loan increases as the period lengthens, and although most banks will have some longer-term loans in their portfolios, they are likely to limit the majority of these to companies they know very well through a direct relationship, and perhaps those companies whose day-to-day financial position they can monitor through current or other short-term accounts. The 'normal' syndicated loan therefore rarely has a repayment programme of more than 5 years, but there are exceptions. The following table shows the distribution of all Euroloan maturities finalized between 1996 and 2000:

Years	1996 (%)	1997 (%)	1998 (%)	1999 (%)	2000 (%)
1	14	20	20	32	51
2	2	4	5	7	5
3	8	7	9	18	10
4	3	2	4	2	1
5	34	31	32	23	19
6	5	–	2	–	1
7	21	16	12	10	4
8–10	7	13	10	6	6
≥11	6	7	6	2	3
	100	100	100	100	100

We can see that maturities of 1 year have increased dramatically from 14% to 51%. This is partly due to the number of loans, especially those financing mergers and acquisitions, which are now structured to have a maturity date of 364 days, with repayment being made by way of a Eurobond issue rather from cash flow generated by the asset being acquired. The same factor has helped to bring down 5 year maturities from 34% to 19%, and 7 year maturities from 21% to 4%. This subject is discussed in detail later in this section.

Revolving facilities

A revolving facility is one which can be used by the borrower to meet short-term cash requirements. It can borrow any amounts (subject to minimum amounts and multiples of, for example, 1 million pounds) and repay them at the end of any interest period. The main difference between a term loan and a revolving facility is that in a term loan, amounts repaid may not be reborrowed, whereas in a revolving facility they may. A revolving facility will always carry a commitment fee to cover periods of non-utilization.

Committed and uncommitted facilities

A committed facility is one in which the lenders are bound to allow the borrower to draw the loan once all the documentary requirements and conditions precedent are fulfilled. An uncommitted loan facility is one in which a bank retains the right not to allow drawdown if the loan would, for whatever reason, not suit the bank's loan portfolio at that time. Obviously, an uncommitted facility would not attract a commitment fee for undrawn amounts.

The uncommitted facility is generally used for bilateral facilities between one bank and a client, and the structure is rarely seen in the syndicated loans market.

Single currency or multi-currency

Whether the loan is denominated in one currency or more makes very little difference to prospective participant banks. The loan may be drawn partly in one currency and partly in another, or there may be an 'alternate currency' option open to the borrower under which it may switch between currencies. As long as the new currency is freely negotiable in the London market this is acceptable.

Repayment profiles

There are three main types of repayment profile, as follows:

- *Amortizing loans*: This is the expression used for loans which have a repayment schedule under which the same amount is repaid on each repayment date. For example, a loan of GBP 5,000,000 may be made for a period of 5 years with 10 semi-annual repayments of GBP 500,000 each commencing 6 months after the date of drawdown.
- *Bullet repayment*: This is the expression used for a term loan of, for example, 3 years which is to be repaid in full in one instalment at the end of the 3 year period.
- *Balloon repayment*: This is the expression used for a loan in which relatively small amounts are repaid regularly during the initial period of the loan, leaving one large repayment on the final repayment date. For example, a loan of GBP 10,000,000 maybe made for 5 years with nine semi-annual repayments of GBP 500,000 commencing 6 months after the date of drawdown. These repayments will total GBP 4,500,000

with 6 months of the loan period remaining, and one final repayment of GBP 5,500,000 will be due on the final maturity date.

Of these three profiles, the amortizing loan is the most commonly seen as the other profiles are only used in special circumstances.

Of course, there are other types of loan facilities which, for example, are subject to annual review and under which the loan is repayable at the end of the loan period if the facility is not renewed.

Repayments via bond issues/acquisition finance

In addition to the repayment profiles described above, there is the loan which is structured to be repaid by a future issue of bonds. This approach reached prominence in the late 1990s to finance large acquisitions quickly, and typically the takeover of another company for a cash consideration.

The background can be that the borrower is planning to make a takeover bid for Company X. To enable it to do so it needs to have a financial package in place from an arranger or, more likely, a group of joint arrangers and underwriters who will provide the initial loan facility prior to general syndication. In this way the loan facility can be provided quickly and confidentially. The borrower is purchasing a long-term asset and therefore it will prudently require long-term finance, and this is more suited to the bond market than the syndicated loan market. However, an issue of bonds takes much longer to arrange than a 'primary' syndicated loan and therefore the loan facility (which, of course, will not be used if the bid is unsuccessful) is used in the first instance. It is structured to have a bullet repayment, or a balloon repayment if the borrower expects to sell off parts of Company X before making the bond issue for the remaining amount.

The most common structure now used consists of a bond issue being made within 364 days, therefore keeping the loan to a short-term basis (thus exploiting loopholes in the capitalization requirements enshrined in the *Basle II Capital Adequacy* guidelines).

There may be a 6 month or a 12 month extension option if conditions in the bond market are unsuitable for the issue, but this extension period would carry a higher interest rate.

From the prospective participant's point of view when the loan comes to general syndication, several issues are raised. First, a basic credit assessment on the borrower. What will its balance sheet look like after it has made the acquisition, merged its balance sheet with that of Company X, and taken on a substantial amount of new debt? Is it paying a premium to acquire Company X, do the fundamental reasons for the takeover make good business sense, and will the new management structure work?

Then we come to the repayment of the loan. Although the period of the loan is stated to be short term, the borrower will need time to sort out the acquisition, possibly sell some subsidiaries which it does not require, and obtain or get confirmation of a post-acquisition rating from the major ratings agencies (Moody's and Standard & Poor's). What will happen to the bond market in this time? If we hit a period of recession and there have been some major corporate failures, the bond market may effectively be dead, the bond issue will have to be delayed or cancelled, and the participants will not receive repayment on time.

Even if the bond market is stable, who will arrange the bond issue? Do they have the necessary experience and placing power to give additional credibility to the loan? Usually in a proposal of the size which we are discussing, the lead arranger and the joint arrangers will have a bond department which would be able to handle these issues, or they would not have received the mandate from the borrower in the first place. In fact, some banks have merged their syndicated loans department with their bonds department so that they can offer a potential borrower a 'one stop' service (although it has to be said that this type of merger does not always work because of differences in business cultures).

We can see that there can be good reasons for banks to shy away from this kind of repayment proposal. And yet, almost without exception, such loans are successfully syndicated. Why? Because the borrower has to be prepared to pay more in interest and fees. All loans are measured in part by the risk/return ratio, and if the return is generous enough, banks can be prepared to participate in a loan in which the proposed repayment is dependent on factors outside their control, especially if they can take comfort from the fact (i.e. convince themselves) that, even if the bond issue is delayed or cancelled, they will still have a decent loan paying a good margin.

The growth of the use of bond issues to repay acquisition finance has had the result of shortening maturities, because the loan is not relying upon cash flow or future sales of unwanted assets. The following table shows the maturity profile of acquisition finance in the Euroloan market from 1997 to 2000.

Years	1997 (%)	1998 (%)	1999 (%)	2000 (%)
1	11	34	40	63
2	1	3	6	6
3	2	2	21	11
5	60	32	21	19
>5	26	29	12	1
	100	100	100	100

It can be seen that in 1997, 86% of loans had a maturity of 5 years or over but this had fallen to 20% in 2000. During the same period, loans with a maturity of one or two tears have risen from 12% to 69%.

Evergreen facilities

An evergreen facility is a facility which is usually given for working capital (i.e. non-specific) purposes, with an annual review. However if, at the time of the review, the lenders wish to cancel the facility despite the fact that no event of default has occurred, they must give the borrower a long period of notice, usually at least 1 year and perhaps 2 years, before the facility may be withdrawn. This is to give the borrower ample time to reorganize its finances at what may be a difficult time.

The evergreen notice period does not apply if an event of default occurs, when repayment on demand can be called for. The financial covenants in the loan agreement therefore need to be tightly drawn so that the borrower does not have too much latitude if it is experiencing difficulties and the banks wish to protect their positions.

Senior debt, mezzanine finance, and subordinated loans

The term senior debt means the full covenant of a borrower to repay a loan. This is the customary type of debt made by a syndicated loan.

Mezzanine finance is known as such because, as a mezzanine floor of a building sits between the ground floor and the first floor, mezzanine finance lies, in terms of priority, beneath the rights of lending banks (particularly if the banks are secured) but above the rights of the shareholders of a company if that company goes into liquidation. Because it carries additional risk, mezzanine finance is avoided by most banks and is more likely to be provided by a venture capital firm, but some specialist lenders can be prepared to make this type of loan, which will carry a higher interest margin. Mezzanine finance can typically be found in the financing packages for management buyouts.

A subordinated loan

Subordinated loans are often made to a company by shareholders, the repayment of which can only be made once all the company's bank debts are fully repaid. The subordinated loan must be shown separately in the company's balance sheet and explained in the notes to the accounts.

Because of its deferred and usually long-term status, the subordinated loan may be regarded as quasi-capital by the company, but banks will not regard it as such. If a subordinated loan is shown in a company's accounts, banks should obtain a copy of the subordinated loan agreement so that they can check that it is worded to their satisfaction, and the loan agreement for the syndicated loan should make it an event of default if any part of the subordinated loan is repaid while the syndicated loan remains outstanding.

Securitization

Securitization refers to the purchase by the borrower of trading assets from another company. The assets can vary widely, but will normally consist of a large number of individual financial receivables which are 'bundled' together and sold as one lot. Both the buyer and the seller are therefore likely to be in the financial services sector. Examples are credit card receivables, mortgages, hire purchase receivables, and leasing receivables. The reason behind the sale by the original owner of the assets is usually to free up its balance sheet and give it the capacity to write new business of the same kind. Conversely, the purchaser will have the capacity to take on the business and probably is under-represented in or new to the particular sector. Normally each 'bundle' will consist of a stream of receivables which each have a similar maturity and repayment profile and will be clear of any record of late payment or non-performance. The purchaser is obtaining the assets quickly and without the need for marketing, and a syndicated loan to finance the acquisition can be structured to match the maturity of the assets. This type of syndicated loan is therefore usually well received in the market. There can, however, be a potential danger to banks which are already lending to the seller of securitized assets. As mentioned above, the assets being sold are usually ones which have no history of late payment or non-performance. If a series of securitizations is made by a company, it could be found that its overall portfolio is deteriorating in quality because it is disposing of its best assets and is retaining those which are not attractive to purchasers.

Therefore the normal loan agreement for a syndicated loan will contain restrictions under which securitizations are restricted or not allowed without the banks' prior permission.

Securitization issues can be made of high risk or poorly performing assets, particularly if a financial institution decides to pull out of a particular sector. These issues can only be sold at a discount and will involve a write-off by the seller. Because the underlying assets are of higher risk, they are not attractive to lending bankers unless they are guaranteed in some way.

Trade finance/pre-export finance

The financing of the flows of capital goods between countries is an extremely important subject to all bankers. Most trade finance transactions are financed by a single bank; here, we will concentrate on the types of loan facility which are regularly syndicated in the London market.

This type of project involves a borrower in a developing country, for example in Africa, for which many banks would not have a country limit, but which produces goods which are readily saleable in the global market. These goods are regularly sold to prime quality purchasers, and an added attraction to banks participating in these loans is that they can also establish a relationship with the purchasers.

As an example, we will look at a base commodity being produced in an African country. If the arranger were to approach the London market with a proposal to finance this commodity by making a loan to the producer, it would find that not only do many banks have no country limits for the country, but if a bank were to take on this country risk (particularly if the transaction extends to more than 1 year), it would immediately have to make a provision against the loan. Yet the underlying proposal is basically sound, so long as it can be structured in a way that will take away the credit risk on the exporting country, and minimize the performance risk.

A typical syndicated loan for pre-export finance of a commodity will normally have the following features:

- The commodity is pre-sold to buyers acceptable to the banks, under fixed price contracts.
- The commodity has usually reached the stage where it is already stored in warehouses, ready for export, and under the control of an internationally known institution such as Société Générale de Surveillance which will agree to act only on the instructions of the agent.
- The goods are insured while they remain in the warehouse, with the policy assigned to the agent.
- The sales contracts are assigned to the agent, and the purchasers pay direct to an offshore account in the name of the agent, thus avoiding any risks of misappropriation or foreign exchange restrictions in the

country of the producer. Most syndicated loans have monthly or quarterly delivery schedules for the goods.
- There is a history of the exporter complying with sales contracts and of the purchasers accepting the quality and quantity of the goods.
- The transactions are short term (less than 1 year) and have acceptable margins and fees.
- There are opportunities for repeat business – the banks which finance 1 year's production are usually invited back for subsequent years.

Some examples of loans which have been syndicated on this basis have been for the following countries and commodities:

- *Jamaica*: sugar
- *Zambia*: copper
- *Ivory Coast*: cocoa
- *Ghana*: cocoa/oil
- *Tanzania*: cotton
- *Uganda*: coffee
- *Malawi*: coffee
- *Angola*: oil
- *Zimbabwe*: cotton/tobacco.

Most central banks do not require their domestic banks to make provisions against financings for emerging economies if the loan is for trade finance purposes and is less than 1 year in duration.

The history of these types of transactions show that they are not only successfully syndicated, but often oversubscribed. This is because banks with an interest in trade finance will normally start by participating at the lowest possible level, probably USD 500,000, but will discover that the structure actually works, and will gradually wish to increase the level of their commitments.

Stock loans

Stock loans can be related to trade finance, as they commonly finance goods which have been imported and are now stored in a warehouse awaiting sale. If they are structured properly, they can be very attractive loan assets.

The ideal structure would be that a debenture is taken over the borrower, incorporating fixed and floating charges over all the company's assets, with a pledge over the goods being financed. However, this is not always possible, and a new Special Purpose Vehicle (SPV) may be set up to be used as the borrower, the assets of which (i.e. the goods being financed) are ring fenced, and the debenture is taken over the SPV. The floating charge in the debenture is vital as the goods being financed will change from time to time.

The goods are warehoused in the agent's name and the warehouse confirms that it will not release the goods except on the instructions of the agent, and that the warehouse has no claims against the borrower (so that the warehouse cannot claim any of the goods if there are, for example, unpaid storage fees). The goods will be stored separately so that they cannot be confused with other goods, and the agent has the right to inspect and value the goods at any time. The goods are insured, with the agent being the party to whom any insurance proceeds are paid. A maximum of perhaps 70% of the purchase price of the goods will be advanced, with the knowledge that their sale value should be much higher, and the agent has the right to call for extra security or a part repayment if the goods fall in value or remain unsold for a specific period.

When the goods are sold, the agent will only authorize their release if the sales proceeds are paid directly to the agent.

Project finance

Project finance is a wide ranging subject. Here, we will concentrate on merely identifying the types of project finance proposals which may come to the syndicated loans market.

Project finance is a generic term for financing of construction of an asset, and whose repayment is obtained from the future cash flows of the facility behind financed. Examples can be an electricity generating station, where the sales of electricity into the grid repay the loan, or the construction of a road which will charge tolls on vehicles using it.

In the UK, project finance has expanded through the advent of the private finance initiative (PFI) under which items that would previously have been financed by the UK government are now financed by bank syndications which rely on the underlying asset for repayment without any government guarantee.

The problems facing a bank's credit committee when assessing such a proposal are that the proposal relies on forecasts and assumptions which may turn out to be flawed or incorrect.

Cost overruns on large projects are common, for example, the construction period may turn out to be longer than envisaged (which will endanger the cash flow even if there are penalty clauses for late completion in the construction contract), and changes to the specifications may be made which have to be agreed quickly by the banks. (Conversely, the projections may be unduly optimistic because they are prepared for inclusion into the information memorandum whose goal, despite the poker-faced disclaimers on the cover, is designed to present the transaction in attractive terms to participating banks in order to enable junior analysts to present the deal with pre-digested and well developed arguments to their credit committee, thereby facilitating the approval process and improving the chances of a successful syndication.)

When the construction is completed, the revenues generated may turn out to be far less than was forecast. Because of the nature of the construction and repayment structure, the financing required is likely to be long term, and in the event of anything going wrong, enormous amounts of management time will need to be spent on trying to rectifying the problems while protecting the bank's position. Indeed, some very successful careers are made by bankers in the loan workout groups, it is, without doubt, a job which will never be made redundant.

A well known project financing which is still failing to meet 'projection targets' some 10 years after its 1994 inauguration is Eurotunnel. This however does not mean Eurotunnel is simply a failure – it is essential to understand the background context to the transaction. What it does mean is that the project was entered into by the Thatcher government for political reasons but the Thatcherite ideology was anathema to the use of public funds in the project (irrespective of arguments for upgrading public infrastructure and expanding trade and the tax base), and thus passed the burden onto the banks, which were more or less expected to provide the funds, akin to paying dues to join a country club. Hence, financial analysts in banks, who typically work on long-term loans not more than 5–7 years in duration extended on commercial criteria understood that they were being asked to finance a national infrastructure project with amortization horizons of at least 20–25 years for the sake of supporting the prevailing ideology. The analysts implicitly understood that the financial projections for Eurotunnel were unrealistic but the ambiguities were to be ignored in an effort for them, as well as the bank, to be seen as 'playing ball'.

Such issues on the subject of project finance projections have become further complicated in 2002–2004 due to the series of accounting scandals which has resulted in a major loss of credibility in accountants' pronouncements and the financial statements they audit (e.g. Enron, or the Euro 15 bn 'hole' in Parmalat of Italy's accounts which had been carried over year to year for 10 years and never spotted by the auditors!), and the dysfunctions of credit rating agencies in accurately assessing risk (as discussed in the US Senate Hearings on the shortcomings of the credit rating agencies in the Enron debacle). Indeed, the reputation of banks knowingly structuring and misrepresenting deals has been covered by the press (see box in page 81). The end result is that projections in the hands of managers 'chasing the deal', have regressed to exercises of illusion and legerdemain.

Such matters however cannot be permitted to dampen the enthusiastic nature of the financial markets, deal originators, and credit committees, especially those in smaller banks who cannot source assets by themselves and thus rely on being invited into syndicated loans in order to build loan portfolios with diversified risks, cultivate their relationship with borrowers, arrangers, and other co-participants (we will never invite you to lunch again!), generate fee income, and meet performance targets, even when the integrity of projections and even financial statements cannot be wholly relied upon.

The timeframe for getting fired for failing to meet sales performance targets after all, is far shorter than waiting for the repayment phase in a project financing, which can be several years down the road. Such cases are extreme but it is important to be able to recognize them for what they are.

But not all project financings end up in this way. If the project is sited overseas there could be a guarantee from the UK government – owned the Export Credits Guarantee Department (ECGD) if there is a British involvement in the construction, or alternatively some kind of government guarantee from the country in which the project is based. And plenty of projects are completed and repaid on schedule, so banks that are happy to lend long term can find the proposals interesting.

One point worth noting is that, as mentioned above, the banks will have to approve any changes to the construction specifications. This is because the construction agreement will form part of the finance documents. The necessary approval (or non-approval) has to be given quickly because the project cannot be held up while one bank with a small participation takes a month to give its decision. Therefore on a proposal which is likely to be well received in the market, the arranger will only invite banks to participate if it knows that they can respond to events quickly, without a long chain of responsibility which has to be followed.

Indeed, in loan workouts, it is not uncommon for recalcitrants to be 'taken out' of the syndication (their share paid off by the other banks) so that a more coordinated and speedy negotiation process can be effected. While smaller banks can adopt the recalcitrant approach as a strategy to exit the transaction, and recoup their losses such behaviour is short termist, as the marketplace keeps track of banks that do not 'play ball' and will avoid them in future (at least until the next syndication where the pressures to fully syndicate an unattractive credit means that an agent bank may well have to again invite the said bank). Moreover, the bank may always have a new manager which means that there is no loss of face in again approaching the bank for a syndication.

Structures used in syndicated loans

The following article illustrates some of the pressures on banks and how they cope with them in an effort to 'nail the deal' and ingratiate themselves with 'important clients'

July 23, 2002
Citigroup Said to Mould Deal to Help Enron Skirt Rules
By Richard A. Oppel Jr. and Kurt Eichenwald

Senior credit officers of Citigroup misrepresented the full nature of a 1999 transaction with Enron in the records of the deal so that the energy company could ignore accounting requirements and hide its true financial condition, according to internal bank documents and government investigators.

The relationship between Enron and its bankers has been a focus of investigative efforts since the company collapsed amid an accounting scandal last December. For months, both Citigroup and J. P. Morgan Chase have been repeatedly criticized by investigators and shareholders' lawyers for structuring billions of dollars of transactions for Enron involving entities with names like Mahonia, Yosemite, Delta and Stoneville Aegean.

The *New York Times* said that bankers intentionally manipulated the written record of their dealings with Enron to allow the company to improperly avoid the requirements of accounting rules and the law, thus keeping USD 125 million in debt off its books.

In the 1999 deal, the records show, the bankers knew that a secret oral agreement they had reached with Enron required that the accounting for the transaction be changed. Instead, investigators said, Citigroup left that side deal out of the written record and allowed Enron to account for the transaction in a way that the bankers knew was improper. In other words, the full terms of the deal were left out of the paperwork, with the result being that anyone reviewing it would have no idea that the accounting treatment being used by Enron was not proper.

A spokesman for Citigroup declined to comment, but he stressed that the bank believed that its dealings with Enron were 'entirely appropriate.'

The transaction and other deals between Enron and the banks are expected to be examined today at a hearing before the Senate Permanent Subcommittee on Investigations. Already, some members of the committee have concluded that the 'Roosevelt' transaction violated accounting rules.

'Citibank was a participant in this accounting deception,' said Senator Carl Levin, Democrat of Michigan and the panel's chairman. The subcommittee's ranking Republican, Susan M. Collins of Maine, said the investigation had found that Citigroup was willing to risk its reputation 'to keep Enron, an important client, happy.'

Mr Bennett, the Enron lawyer, said the current criticisms by Congress were a result of political pressure to crack down on the appearance of corporate wrongdoing. 'What we have here is an incredible amount of revisionist history, which is motivated by the upcoming election,' he said. 'Most of the problems – not all of them – are things that have been legal and have been acceptable.'

Copyright 2002 The New York Times Company

Aircraft finance

These financings of individual aircraft tend to be long term, commonly at least 12 years, and are therefore seen as a very specialized sector. They combine macro-economic factors such as the number of passenger or freight flights per annum, together with micro-economic factors such as the fixture stability of an airline, the statutory periodic airworthiness certificates required on individual aircraft and the likelihood of fixture changes to regulations for factors such as noise pollution, and the future valuation and/or usefulness of an airplane if it is no longer required by the airline which commissioned its construction.

Aircraft finance loans are regularly seen in the syndicated loans market but are generally confined to participants who specialize in the sector.

Ship construction finance

These loans can be very complex. The borrower will be the shipyard at which the vessel is being built, with repayments coming from contracted payments made by the purchaser. For large and expensive vessels, loan drawings are normally made in accordance with the production schedule, and repayments are made as certain stages in the construction are reached and accepted by the purchaser. The underlying risk is on the shipyard performing its duties to a good standard and in time with an extremely tightly drawn schedule.

Now that the UK shipbuilding industry is virtually non-existent, syndicated loan proposals are most likely to be received for overseas shipbuilders, and the participants will include a good percentage of banks incorporated in the country of the shipbuilder.

Non-recourse loans

Some companies are well enough respected that they can negotiate a loan which relies completely on the underlying project, which is perceived to be strong enough to 'stand on its own feet' without recourse back to the borrower should anything go wrong. In these situations a SPV will act as borrower and the assets involved in the project will be ring fenced and charged to the syndicate as security. Occasionally, the bank syndicate will receive a profit share when the project is completed. The types of loan involved can vary, but an example would be a property development in which the completed property has been pre-sold.

Standby credits

A standby credit facility acts as a type of guarantee to a company which has a corporate bond programme under which it will issue bonds or corporate paper to finance its longer-term finance requirements. The standby credit is in place so that the company can draw against it if it is unable to access the bond market under this programme. The reasons for the unavailability of bond issues could be that there is general market disruption, or because the company itself has been downgraded by the ratings agencies and is now rated as non-investment grade. Standby credit facilities are almost always short term, and subject to annual review. The banks will receive a fairly small commitment fee while the facility remains undrawn, but if it is utilized the interest rate is quite high because at that time the risk to the lenders could be high.

Property finance

The property market as a whole is cyclical and the value of a property can fall dramatically and very quickly for macro-economic reasons. Therefore, property financing is not attractive to all banks, particularly the London branches of some foreign banks which may feel that UK valuations are too high and are vulnerable to a downturn. However, banks that do have an interest in the sector tend to be prepared to lend large amounts on the right proposals. syndicated loans for property purposes are therefore not particularly common, and loans that are syndicated generally tend to be arranged between a few banks on a club basis rather than being put to the general syndication market. There is generally a 'loan to value' maximum applied which will depend upon the type of financing required but which is usually around 60%.

The outlines of the different types of property loans are:

- *Investment property*: An existing building is let to one or more tenants who will have leases which are 'fully repairing' and the tenant is responsible for the upkeep, decoration and any repairs to the property. There will be rent reviews, normally every 5 years, which will be 'upwards only', i.e. the rent roll will increase and not decrease. The property will be charged to the banks by way of first legal mortgage and the banks will also have charges over the rental receivables and the proceeds of any insurance claims. The banks have to satisfy themselves on the covenant of the tenants and the period of their leases – if one tenant leaves, can another of sufficient quality be found?
- *Property construction*: This can relate to a single office or industrial property, or an estate of new houses. The finance is usually drawn down in stage payments against architects' certificates which confirm the amount and value of work completed. The land and property is again charged to the banks by way of first legal mortgage, with a charge over the benefit of the insurance policies.

If the proposal is for a single industrial or office building which is to be sold at completion, it may be that the property is pre-sold before construction starts. In this case the banks will have to consider the ability of the purchaser to complete the purchase, and they will take a charge over the sale agreement. If the completed property is not pre-sold, the proposal is considered to be speculative and therefore far less attractive.

If the building is not to be sold but retained and let, the considerations of whether or not the completed building is pre-let will apply, and if it is not pre-let the suitability of the building attracting suitable tenants will have to be assessed.

If the proposal is for new houses, the banks will have to consider whether or not they will saleable at the required price on completion, and will receive estate agents' opinions on this.

Vodafone AirTouch

Why do companies borrow huge amounts? One company which set a record for borrowing is the British telecommunications company Vodafone AirTouch. Vodafone AirTouch was the largest borrower in the global syndicated loans market during the year 2000, with a total of USD 39.7 bn raised in three transactions. In this case study we will examine the circumstances which led to this massive amount being raised.

During 1999 and 2000 Vodafone transformed itself from being the largest mobile phone business in the UK to being the largest in the world, with approximately 93 million customers world-wide. In terms of market capitalization, it is the largest company in the FTSE 100, and it is one of the 10 largest companies in the world. It reached this position by a series of unprecedented acquisitions financed by a mixture of syndicated loans and bond issues.

Vodafone was floated from the UK-based Racal Group in 1988, and in the period up to 1998 it completed a number of Euroloans and Eurobond issues to finance some relatively modest acquisitions. Then, in 1999 Vodafone announced a bid for AirTouch Communications of the USA, which it successfully completed at a cost of USD 65.5 bn. This was, at the time, one of the largest cross-border M&A transactions ever made, and it was backed by one of the world's biggest syndicated loans; a USD 14 bn Euroloan launched in May 1999 and arranged by 11 banks. Subsequently reduced to USD 10 bn, this loan was one of the first to be structured with repayment (or 'takeout') to be made within 364 days by a Eurobond issue.

This has now become normal practice for jumbo M&A deals, since taking advantage of an M&A opportunity requires speed, which a syndicated loan can provide far better than a bond or equity issue with its stringent disclosure requirements.

The arrangers retained their participations, so general syndication was not required. The loan was duly repaid by means of a Euro 1.5 bn, 7 years bond issue that September, and Vodafone was established as a major borrower.

At the end of 1999, Vodafone announced another major bid, this time for its European joint venture partner Mannesman AG of Germany. This produced great hostility in Germany, particularly from Mannesman's board and employees, but the bid was ultimately successful at Euro 155 bn. Although the offer was all shares, with Mannesman shares being exchanged for Vodafone shares, a supporting syndicated loan to refinance Mannesman's borrowings was underwritten in December 1999 and brought to the general market in February 2000.

At the underwriting stage, this was for EUR 30 bn, and 11 banks underwrote approximately EUR 2.7 bn each. These were banks which already had a close relationship with Vodafone, and consisted of ABN Amro, Bank of America, Banque Nationale de Paris, Barclays Capital, Citibank, Goldman Sachs, Greenwich NatWest., ING Bark, National Australia Bank, Toronto Dominion, and Warburg Dillon Read.

Just before the underwritten loan was brought to general syndication, it was reduced to EUR 25 bn by a USD 5.25 bn global bond issue – the largest ever bond issue made by a UK company. The total EUR 25 bn consisted of:

1 a revolving credit of EUR 10 bn, 364 days with 6 months term out option,

Structures used in syndicated loans

2 a revolving credit of EUR 7.5 bn, 364 days with 1 year term out option,
3 a revolving credit of EUR 7.5 bn, for 3 years.

At syndication, the loan was massively oversubscribed with commitments being received for EUR 65 bn. This, plus the original commitments of the underwriters, meant that a total of EUR 95 bn was raised – the largest amount ever seen to date in the global loan markets.

The loan was subsequently reduced to EUR 17 bn in March 2000 following a reduction in Mannesman's borrowing requirements.

In May 2000 Vodafone came back to the market following its purchase of the largest available 'next generation' 3G licence for GBP 5.96 bn. It raised a USD 5 bn 364 days loan facility, as well as raising USD 3.75 in floating rate notes, Yen 60 bn in bonds, and increased its medium term note facility from EUR 3 bn to 8 bn.

Vodafone, however, now changed its strategy in relation to the loan. Instead of mandating a number of its relationship banks, it arranged the deal itself on a club basis. The loan was priced at a 'competitive' (i.e. less than generous) 35bp over LIBOR with a front end fee of 2.5bp, and 15 banks participated.

Vodafone is now committed to a major programme of divestment to repay debt but also to give room for possible future acquisitions if the right opportunities occur.

The main reasons for Vodafone's ability to raise spectacular amounts of money were:

- confidence in the company and its management,
- confidence that the deals being considered made sound commercial sense,
- confidence in the telecoms sector and its continuing growth,
- confidence that the loans were well structured and would be repaid on time and without problems.

Syndicated Lending

It is interesting to look at Vodafone's accounts over the last 5 years, and how the acquisitions have affected them:

To 31 March GBP mn	1997	1998	1999	2000	2001
Profit and loss a/c					
Turnover	1749	2471	3360	7873	15,004
Pre-tax profit	539	650	935	1349	(8095)
Balance sheet					
Intangibles	147	138	329	22,206	108,839
Fixed assets	1260	1572	2150	6307	10,586
Fixed investments	519	202	372	122,338	34,950
Stocks	19.7	28.9	44.7	190	316
Debtors	434	547	741	2138	4095
Cash, securities	41.8	15.3	6.10	189	13,279
Creditors short	1013	1426	1530	4441	12,377
Creditors long	580	696	1189	6567	11,906
Preferance shares, minorities	58.6	97.0	110	1527	2389
Capital and reserves	770	283	815	140,833	145,393
Market capitalization	8539	19,285	35,674	213,749	125,474

The market sentiment for the jumbo loans which Vodafone raised in 1999 and 2000 has now changed. Following the growth of the mobile phone market across the board, most banks are now heavily committed to a range of different borrowers in the sector. The upwardly-spiralling growth in mobile phone users seems to be tailing off a little, and questions are now being asked about the amounts telecom companies paid to buy new licences.

A new jumbo loan would probably still be achievable, but with far more difficulty than in the recent past, and at a higher return to the participating banks. But in this period Vodafone and its bankers gave a good example of how a borrower can use groundbreaking financial strategies involving a blend of different debt markets to raise enormous amounts of funding in a very short time.

Chapter 6

The loan agreement

Any loan made by a bank will be governed by a loan agreement setting out the terms and conditions of the loan. It is signed by the bank and countersigned by the borrower to signify its agreement with the terms and conditions as stated. The loan agreement can take many different styles, and each bank – and the firm of solicitors it uses – can have its own house style. The loan agreement can be as short as one page and still be legally binding so long as the integral parts of the loan are identified and agreed. In a basic loan agreement these are:

- The amount of the loan
- The purpose
- The period
- The rate of interest plus any fees payable by the borrower
- How and when repayment will be made
- Any security.

In a syndicated loan facility these integral terms are expanded greatly by the addition of other clauses. This is because, the syndicated loan agreement is intended to cover every eventuality which may occur while all or part of the loan remains outstanding. In the event of a default or other irregularity in the loan, it could be virtually impossible for the agent to manage a group of what might be 50 or 60 banks, each with their own opinions and priorities, unless the loan agreement specifically states in advance what actions may be taken. The loan agreement in a syndicated loan is therefore very detailed and is usually drawn up by large firms of solicitors. Indeed, some participant banks have lists of solicitors, one of which must be used to draw up and opine on the loan agreement or they will not participate in the loan.

The additional clauses which are added to the integral parts of the loan agreement generally fall into two categories: administrative and credit. The administrative clauses set out such things as how and when drawdowns may be made, how the rate of interest is set and for which periods, etc. The credit clauses set out obligations which the borrower takes on such as financial covenants, negative covenants such as not giving security to other lenders, and warranties, etc.

Each syndicated loan facility is an individual transaction and the loan agreement will be drawn up to reflect the mandate which the arranger has received from the borrower for the particular purpose and circumstances of the loan. The arranger will appoint a firm of solicitors to represent the participating banks, and the borrower will also appoint solicitors to represent its own interests. If security is to be given by a third party, such as a guarantee, the guarantor may also appoint solicitors. The different firms must work together with the arranger to produce a document which is acceptable to all parties. Although all cases are different, the loan agreement for a syndicated loan would normally contain the following clauses.

The preamble

The preamble is a short statement which sets out the date of the loan agreement and the names of the various parties to the loan, and gives them definitions such as 'borrower'. The participating banks will not be individually named here, but referred to as the banks set out in a schedule to the loan agreement. A typical preamble would read as follows:

This agreement is dated the ... date ... and made between:

1 name of borrower (the 'borrower')
2 name of guarantor (the 'guarantor')
3 name of arranger ... (the 'arranger')

4 the financial institutions listed in Schedule 1 (the 'lenders')
5 name of agent ... as agent of the lenders (the 'agent').

Whereas it is agreed as follows.

Definitions

This clause gives reference definitions to all the key components of the loan agreement. The clause is usually one of the lengthiest clauses in the loan agreement because it must give precise and detailed definitions to avoid any subsequent argument or confusion over any of the terms used. Once a term is defined in this clause, only this reference definition will be used throughout the loan agreement, and it will be given capital opening letters to signify that its definition is shown in the definitions clause.

A typical definitions clause would include most or all of the following headings, and possibly more. The explanations given here are simple and brief and are not intended to give the longer and more precise definitions which would appear in the actual loan agreement. They appear in alphabetical order.

Additional Guarantor	a company, possibly a new subsidiary of the borrower, which becomes a guarantor after the signing of the loan agreement.
Affiliate	a definition of the subsidiary companies and the holding company of the borrower.
Agent's spot rate of exchange	a definition of the calculation of the rate at which the agent can convert different currencies which may be used in the loan.
Authorization	a wide ranging definition of what form an authorization may take.
Availability period or commitment period	a definition of the period during which the loan may be drawn. It usually commences on the date of signature of the loan agreement and ends on the termination date, which is usually within 3 months from the date of signature, although the

	period can be lengthened in, for example, project finance loans.
Available commitment	a definition of the amount of the loan which may still be drawn, in terms of each lender's individual commitment.
Available facility	the total amount of the loan which may still be drawn.
Base currency	the currency of the loan.
Base currency Amount	the equivalent amount in the base currency of any amounts in different currencies.
Break costs	a definition of the calculation of the amount which each lender can claim from the borrower if, due to a prepayment of all or part of the loan, the lender suffers a loss of income or profit.
Business day	the days during which payments or foreign exchange transactions under the loan facility may be made.
Commitment	in relation to each lender, the amount of its commitment less any amounts already drawn.
Commitment period	see Availability period.
Compliance Certificate	a certificate to be received from the borrower showing that the financial covenants of the loan facility are being adhered to, and the bases of calculation.
Event of default	any of the events of default specified in the loan agreement.
Facility	the facility of which the terms and conditions are set out in this loan agreement.
Facility amount	the limit of the loan facility. (NB: This may alternatively be defined as total commitments.)
Fee letter	a letter detailing fees payable in respect of the loan facility. It may be from the borrower to the arranger, from the arranger to the lenders, or from the borrower to the agent.
Finance document	the loan agreement, the fee letter, and any other similar document.

The loan agreement

Finance party	an inclusive term for the arranger, the agent, and any lender or security party.
Financial indebtedness	any indebtedness of the borrower and/or the guarantor in respect of moneys borrowed by any method, including bond or note issues, any other commercial transactions having the commercial effect of a borrowing, plus guarantees and indemnities.
GAAP	generally accepted accounting principles.
Group	the borrower and its affiliates.
Information Memorandum	the document prepared by the arranger in consultation with the borrower prior to syndication of the loan, giving information on the borrower and the structure of the loan facility.
Interest payment Date	the last day of each interest period, when interest for that period is payable.
Interest period	a definition of the interest periods available to the borrower and, in the event of a default, default interest periods chosen by the agent.
Lender	this definition amplifies the original lenders to include any other subsequent lender.
LIBOR	the definition of the London Inter Bank offered rate and how and when it is calculated. (NB: LIBOR may be replaced by EURIBOR in loans denominated in Euro, and if the loan is syndicated in another financial centre, such as Paris, the abbreviation would be PIBOR and if in Singapore, SIBOR.)
Loan	the aggregate principal amount of drawings made under this loan agreement.
Majority lenders	a group of lenders whose advances and remaining commitments total a defined percentage of the loan, usually 66⅔%.
Mandatory costs	a definition of the calculation made by the agent of any additional costs to lenders incurred in complying with Bank of England or other regulatory body requirements. The basis of

Margin	the margin above LIBOR applicable to the loan.
material adverse change	the occurrence of any event (in addition to the events of default) which, in the opinion of the lenders, may jeopardize the due repayment of the loan. (NB: Some borrowers may not agree to the inclusion of this clause, on the grounds that it gives too wide a scope for the lenders to call for repayment.)
Month	a definition of a calendar month, with particular relevance to interest periods. The definition is expanded to cover situations such as a month ending on a day which is not a business day.
Obligor	the borrower or guarantor, including any additional guarantors.
Optional currency	a currency, other than the base currency, in which transactions under the terms and conditions of the loan agreement may be made, and the conditions (such as it being freely convertible) under which a currency may become an optional currency.
Original financial statements	the latest audited accounts of an obligor at the time of the signing of the loan agreement. These are referred to because they are the accounts upon which the lenders have based their credit decisions.
Party	a party to this loan agreement, including permitted successors in title, assigns, and transferees.
Qualifying lender	the definition of a bank to which one lender may transfer all or part of its participation in the loan facility.
Quotation day	the beginning of an interest period, for which value date an interest rate is quoted.
Reference banks	a small number of lenders who will give their individual quotation of LIBOR when a new

(calculation will normally be set out in a schedule to the loan agreement.)

	interest period and rate is to be set. (NB: The practice of using reference banks has now largely been replaced by using a screen rate.)
Repayment, repayment schedule, and repayment instalment	the programme and structure for repayment of the loan.
screen rate	the Telerate, Reuters, or other screen page number which will be used to determine LIBOR when a new interest rate and period is to be set.
Sterling, USD, etc.	a definition of the appropriate currency, which will normally be the base currency.
Subsidiary	a definition of a subsidiary company.
tax	a definition of any present or future tax levied on the borrower, particularly relevant to withholding tax.
Termination date	the last day of the availability period or commitment period. If the loan is not fully drawn by this date, any undrawn commitments will lapse.
Total commitments	the total commitments of all the lenders as at the date of signing, i.e. the facility limit. (NB: This may alternatively be defined as facility amount.)
Transfer certificate	the form of words to be used if one lender transfers all or part of its participation to another bank. The full wording is usually set out in a schedule to the loan agreement.
Unpaid sum	any amount of capital or interest due and payable but which has not been paid by an Obligor.
Utilization	a drawing under the loan facility.
Utilization request	an application for a drawdown by the borrower. The full wording will be set out in a schedule to the loan agreement.

The definitions will sometimes be followed by an interpretations or constructions sub-clause, where certain words will be explained for the sake of absolute certainty. The interpretations are usually self-explanatory.

The facility

This section of the loan agreement sets out the type and limit of the facility to be provided to the borrower by the lenders, and the rights and obligations assumed by the lenders in doing so. A typical loan agreement would contain the following clauses.

The facility

Subject to the terms of this agreement, the lenders make available to the borrower a multi-currency term loan facility in an aggregate amount equal to the total commitments.

The term total commitments has already been defined as the facility limit.

Lenders' rights and obligations

This sub-clause states:

- The obligations of the lenders are several (i.e. individual and not interdependent); that a failure by one lender to perform its obligations does not affect the obligations of the other lenders; that no lender is responsible for the obligations of another lender.
- That each lender is making a direct loan to the borrower; therefore it does not have to sue via the agent if it decides not to do so, although with syndicated loans it would be unusual for a bank to take individual action.
- That each lender may separately enforce its rights except as otherwise stated in the loan agreement, i.e. if for some reason the loan agreement should become ineffective, the lenders could independently pursue the repayment of their advances, but otherwise they may only act under the terms of the loan agreement.

Purpose

This clause states the purpose of the loan facility, and states that the lenders do not have a responsibility to ensure that the loan will only be used for these purposes. The purpose may be specific or it may be quite general, e.g. for working capital purposes. If the purpose is specific, for example the purchase of a new fixed asset, then the remainder of the loan agreement will reflect that purpose in the terms and conditions and, perhaps, security. The loan agreement for a general purpose loan is likely to contain less specific or less direct provisions.

Conditions precedent

Before the loan may be drawn, the agent must be able to confirm to the participants that it has received the items listed in this clause which, if lengthy, may be set out in a schedule to the loan agreement. They are likely to include:

- A copy of the Memorandum and Articles of Association (or other constitutional documents) of the borrower, certified as being true and up to date.
- A certified copy of a board resolution approving the loan agreement and any other related documents such as security documents, and authorizing named offers to sign them on behalf of the borrower and to operate the loan account.
- Similar documents from any guarantor or other third party giving security.
- Written legal opinions by the English and, if appropriate, overseas legal advisers to the agent and the lenders.
- All fees which are due to be paid at or before the date of signature of the loan agreement.
- Any security and ancillary documents.
- If the borrower is registered overseas, the written agreement of a process agent to accept suit on behalf of the borrower.
- Any other requirement applicable to this particular syndicated loan.

In addition, by signing the loan agreement the borrower confirms that the representations and warranties contained in the loan agreement are true and correct at the time of drawdown, and that no event of default or potential event of default has occurred.

There may also be further conditions relating to the loan being drawn in optional currencies, and if the loan is to be drawn in more than one instalment, a maximum number of instalments may be stated.

Utilization

This section deals with the drawdown of the loan and will state that a drawdown request, which is irrevocable, must be received by the agent in the form set out in a schedule to the loan agreement before the end of the termination Period. It will state the currency in which the drawdown is to be made and will give the selection of the initial interest period made by the borrower. It will advise the agent where the funds are to be paid and on which date.

Prior to the drawdown date, the agent will advise the participants that the conditions precedent are fulfilled and a drawdown request has been received, and will advise each participant of the amount of its participation to be paid on the drawdown date. The participants will then pay the appropriate amount to the agent and the agent will make one payment of the total amount to the borrower.

Repayment

This clause will specify the repayment structure of the syndicated loan. There are three main types of repayment profile and their colloquial names (which are not used in the loan agreement) are:

- *Amortizing loans*: This is the expression used for loans which have a repayment schedule under which the same amount is repaid on each repayment date. For example, a loan of GBP 5,000,000 may be made for a period of 5 years with 10 semi-annual repayments of GBP 500,000 each commencing 6 months after the date of drawdown.
- *Balloon repayment*: This is the expression used for a loan in which relatively small amounts are repaid regularly during the initial period of the loan, leaving one large repayment on the final repayment date. For example, a loan of GBP 5,000,000 may be made for 5 years with four semi-annual repayments of GBP 125,000 commencing 6 months

after the date of drawdown. These repayments will total GBP 500,000 with 6 months of the loan period remaining, and one final repayment of GBP 4,500,000 will be due on the final maturity date.
- **Bullet repayment**: This is the expression used for a term loan of, for example, 3 years which is to be repaid in full in one instalment at the end of the 3 year period.

Loan type	Year 1	Year 2	Year 3	Year 4	Year 5	Total
Amortizing	1000	1000	1000	1000	1000	5000
Balloon	125	125	125	125	4500	5000
Bullet	0	0	5000	n.a.	n.a.	5000

In each of the above cases, we are referring only to the principal amount of the syndicated loan. Interest must be paid at the end of each interest period, which are normally set at 1, 3, or 6 months at the borrower's option. On very rare occasions, accrued interest may be rolled up and added to the principal amount of the loan, but this is generally considered to be unacceptable to banks as the non-payment of interest is one of the triggers which can necessitate a bank to make a loss provision against a loan.

Of the three types of repayment profile referred to above, banks would generally prefer to see an amortizing loan, as their exposure is steadily reduced and they can measure the progress of the loan throughout its life and perhaps see any early warning signs if the borrower is experiencing problems in adhering to the repayment schedule. A bullet or balloon repayment structure would normally only be used for a special reason. The interest cost to the borrower is also higher in bullet and balloon repayment profiles as the debt burden remains high for a longer period (the loan is said to have a longer average life).

Other less usual repayment profiles can be used and adapted to the particular requirements of a loan transaction, such as a holiday period where repayments do not start until a relatively long period has passed after drawdown, or a sawtooth repayment under which repayment amounts may fluctuate upwards and downwards. These examples would be structured to fit the anticipated cash flow of the borrower from an asset being acquired by means of the loan.

The loan agreement will state whether or not any amounts repaid may be reborrowed; usually in a term loan they may not. If reborrowing is permitted, the loan facility is known as a revolving loan facility and will be referred to as such in the preamble, and the terms under which the reborrowing may be made will be defined in the definitions clause.

Prepayment

This clause covers two topics; prepayment when called for by the lenders, and prepayment made voluntarily by the borrower. It is not intended to cover acceleration caused by an event of default.

The agent may call for prepayment if the agent is advised by a participant that it has become illegal for it to continue to participate in the loan. The borrower must then repay that bank's participation, and any undrawn commitment for that bank will be cancelled. The agent will normally attempt to find a replacement participant.

The borrower may normally cancel any amounts which have not been drawn by giving the agent notice that it wishes to do so. (This could result from, for example, the borrower realizing that it has negotiated a higher facility limit than has proved necessary, or because it has received a new loan at a lower interest cost.) This cancellation is irrevocable.

The borrower may make a voluntary repayment if it gives notice to the agent. The loan agreement will specify what notice period must be given, and will normally state that the repayment must be made at the end of an interest period; otherwise the borrower will be liable for any break costs suffered by the lenders. Any notice of prepayment is irrevocable and the amount repaid may not be reborrowed.

Some loan agreements state that prepayment by the borrower is not permitted. Thus it would need unanimous agreement by the lenders to allow prepayment to be made.

Interest rate

This clause sets out how the interest on the loan is dealt with. It will normally contain the following sub-clauses:

- *Calculation of interest*: The interest rate charged will be the total of the margin, the LIBOR rate for the relevant interest period, and any applicable mandatory costs. These terms have all been defined in the definitions clause. Interest on loans denominated in sterling is calculated on the basis of a 365 day year, and in other currencies on the basis of a 360 day year.
- *Payment of interest*: Interest must be paid on the last day of each interest period. The agent will advise the borrower of the amount in advance so that payment can be made on the appropriate value date.
- *Default interest (sometimes known as penalty interest)*: If the borrower fails to pay any amount on its due date, the margin will be increased by a percentage rate (often one per cent per annum) stated here on the overdue amount from the date of non-payment until payment is made. Interest periods for the amount overdue will be selected by the agent and the interest will be compounded at the end of each interest period. This interest is payable on-demand made by the agent. The increased interest rate is notified to the borrower and the lenders by the agent.
- *Interest periods*: The borrower has the ability to select interest periods, which would typically be of 1, 3, or 6 months duration. It must give written notice of the rate selected to the agent by a specified period (normally 1 or 2 days) before the beginning of the next interest period. If it fails to do so, the agent may select a period specified here, normally 3 months.

An interest period must end on a business day (i.e. not a Saturday, Sunday, or Bank Holiday). If it does not, the last day will automatically be changed to the next business day in that month or, if there is not one in that month, to the preceding business day in that month. For example, if the expiry of an existing interest period is the 25 June and the borrower chooses a new interest period of 1 month, it may be that 25 July is a Saturday; therefore the new interest period would automatically be extended to Monday 27 July. However, if the existing interest period ends on 30 June and 30 July is a Saturday, the next interest period would not be extended to Monday 1 August, but would instead go back to Friday 29 July to keep the expiry date in the same month. The reasons for this are:

(a) to defer the interest payment date into a new month may take it into a new reporting period which could distort reporting figures,

(b) rate fixing at a month end can sometimes be distorted by macro-economic or other influences which cause rates to fluctuate outside normal market rates.

If more than one drawdown has been made, the interest periods for the individual advances will normally have to be matched so that eventually the whole amount if the loan can be rolled over in one amount.

- *Market disruption*: The level of LIBOR for any interest period is determined either by use of reference banks or by a screen rate; these are both defined in the definitions clause. However, it may be that due to some major economic event, the market is disrupted and a true level of LIBOR cannot be ascertained by whichever of these means has been selected in the loan agreement. In this case, the agent will enter into negotiations with the borrower, for a period of up to 30 days, to agree an alternative basis for determining the rate to be charged. In these negotiations, the agent will obviously consult the individual lenders to discover their respective costs of borrowing, but whatever rate is agreed between the agent and the borrower is binding upon all the lenders.

If one lender, due to its individual circumstances, finds that its own cost of funding is materially above the rate of LIBOR quoted, it may advise the agent of this and the agent will advise the borrower (and the other lenders) that it must pay an increased margin to that bank on the amount of its participation. However, this would obviously impair the whole basis of the syndicated loan, and so the agent only has to comply with this requirement if the percentage commitment of that lender is above a predetermined (and high) percentage of the loan, or if a group of lenders whose combined commitments come to that percentage, all make the same claim. Thus, for example, if a syndicate consisted of 60% UK based banks which were all hit by a market disruption which did not affect banks based in other countries, this would be a consideration deemed to be important enough to affect the basis of the interest calculation of the whole of the loan, whereas if only one bank with a commitment of, for example, only 2% of the total loan facility were to be the only bank affected, it would not.

Fees

This clause sets out the fees payable on the syndicate loan facility. Fees are paid by the borrower to the agent, who then distributes them amongst the lenders. As we have already seen, the amounts and types of fees can vary from facility to facility, but some of the types most usually seen are as follows.

Commitment fee

When a bank commits to lend in a syndicated loan facility, it assumes a risk and applies this against its overall loan portfolio even though the loan is not yet drawn, for this the bank wishes to receive a measure of compensation although it will accept that because it is not yet on risk, the return will not be as high as it would had the loan been drawn. This is settled by the payment of a relatively small commitment fee. This fee is calculated from the date of signature of the loan agreement until the date at which the loan is drawn down in full, or the end of the commitment period (the termination date) if the loan is ultimately not fully drawn. If the loan is drawn in more than one tranche, the commitment fee continues to be calculated on the undrawn amount. The commitment fee will typically be fixed at a level of around one eighth per cent per annum, and is paid quarterly or around the last drawdown date or the termination date.

Arrangement fee

This is a fee paid by the borrower to the arranger for arranging the syndicated loan facility. It is usually calculated as a percentage of the amount of the loan rather than a flat fee. It will be paid either at the date the mandate is awarded to the arranger, or upon signature of the loan agreement. The arrangement fee is sometimes known as the Praecipium. Theoretically the arranger is free to retain all of this fee, but usually it distributes a part to the lenders as a front end fee.

Front end fee

This is the colloquial term for the fee a lender will receive for participating in a syndicated loan facility. In the loan agreement it may be called a management fee or simply a fee. It is based upon the percentage of the total loan which the participant commits to provide, and different levels of commitment receive different levels of this fee. As an example, banks committing at a level between 1 million pounds and 5 million pounds may receive a front end fee of one sixteenth per cent, banks committing to between 5 million and 10 million may receive one eighth per cent, and banks committing between 10 million and 15 million may receive three sixteenths per cent. The fee is payable at or around the date of signature of the loan agreement.

The front end fee may not appear in the loan agreement; instead, it may be covered in a separate fee letter between the arranger and the participant. This can be because the arranger has negotiated one overall fee to be paid to itself, and distributes an undisclosed portion of this to the participants. The borrower will not know how much of its fee the arranger has had to give up, and the participants will not know the amount of the fee the arranger is retaining.

Agency fee

The agency fee is payable to the agent by the borrower for conducting the management of the syndicated loan, and is payable annually throughout the duration of the loan. It is retained in full by the agent. The amount and details of the agency fee, and any expenses of the agent to be reimbursed by the borrower, are confidential between the borrower and the agent and they are therefore not set out in the loan agreement but are contained in a separate fee letter which forms part of the finance documents.

The fee letters mentioned in sub-clauses (c) and (d) above fall within the definition of the facility documentation and so any non-payment of one of these fees will constitute a potential event of default, even though at the time of signature of the loan agreement their terms are not generally known.

Taxes and other deductions

Withholding and other taxes indemnity

This lengthy and technical clause is inserted to ensure that any deductions by way of tax or other impositions binding on the borrower are borne by the borrower and not by the lenders. When the arranger submits it bid for the mandate for the syndicated loan, it will usually state that the interest margin is quoted free and clear of taxes and other deductions. If, for example, the borrower should subsequently be subjected to withholding tax on interest payments, the participants will not wish to see their interest margin reduced. The borrower therefore indemnifies the lenders that it will make good any deductions it is forced to make by paying an increased amount so that the lenders receive the original due amount.

Increased costs

When a lender makes a commitment in a syndicated loan it does so on the basis of a known and calculated return on the risk it is assuming. If, subsequent to the date of signature of the loan agreement, the regulatory authorities of the lender impose any new regulations which will decrease this return, the lender will not be willing to bear a cost outside its own control which would alter the risk/return assessment which the participant made. The borrower therefore indemnifies the lenders that, subject to certain stated conditions, it will reimburse the lenders' additional costs or reduced returns in this respect.

Other indemnities

There may be other indemnities from the borrower to the lenders, such as:

- *Currency indemnity*: The borrower indemnifies the lenders against the currency exchange erects of any judgement made against the borrower being in a different currency to the base currency.
- *Expenses*: The borrower indemnifies the lenders for costs and expenses resulting from an event of default or changes to the facility structure.

- *The agent*: The borrower indemnifies the agent against any costs it may incur following a potential or reported event of default.
- *Mitigation*: In consideration of sub-clauses (a), (b), and (c) above, the agent and the lenders agree to mitigate their actions – in other words they will not spend inordinate amounts of money on minor matters just because they know that the borrower will be responsible for payment of the costs.

Guarantee

The borrowers of syndicated loans are, almost without exception, corporate bodies and therefore it is quite usual that the borrower will need to be guaranteed by other members of the same group of companies. Nowadays the guarantee is usually incorporated in the loan agreement rather than being a separate document.

At this point it is worth examining the difference between a guarantee and an indemnity. Under a guarantee, the guarantor agrees with the bank that if the borrower does not meet a legally binding obligation to the bank, then the guarantor will meet it. Thus the guarantor's liability is secondary and collateral, and the guarantor only becomes liable if the borrower defaults.

Under an indemnity, the indemnifier agrees with the bank that he will meet a legally binding obligation of the borrower on a primary basis. The indemnifier is himself immediately liable, and his liability does not depend upon the validity of the borrower's obligation or a default by the borrower.

A typical guarantee will incorporate the following terms and conditions.

Guarantee and indemnity

The guarantee is irrevocable and unconditional. If there is more than one guarantor, their liabilities are joint and several (in other words, the agent can sue just one guarantor for the whole of the debt or any number of them individually, and if one guarantor does not pay the others cannot claim that this is a reason for them not to pay). The guarantor guarantees the performance of the borrower. It undertakes that if the borrower does not pay any amount when due, the guarantor shall immediately on demand do so. It indemnifies the lenders that even if the guarantee becomes invalid, unenforceable or illegal, it will immediately on demand pay the amount due.

Continuing guarantee

The guarantee is a continuing security and extends until all amounts due to the lenders are repaid.

Waiver of defences

The guarantee is not affected by any waiver or consent given to the borrower, any variation of other security, any change of the status of the guarantor, any changes to any of the finance documents or their becoming unenforceable, or any insolvency or similar proceedings against any party.

Immediate recourse

The lenders do not have to proceed against any other party or security before calling the guarantee.

Appropriations

Any funds received by the lenders under the guarantee or any other finance document do not have to be applied in reduction of the loan but may be held in a separate suspense account. This will enable the lenders, in the event of the insolvency of the borrower, to claim for the full amount of the loan in the liquidation proceedings in case only a reduced percentage of total debts is available to the borrower's creditors.

No security

The guarantor may not take any security or payment from the borrower in respect of the guarantee until all amounts due to the lenders have been completely discharged. This is because the lenders do not want the borrower to charge assets which may otherwise be available to the lenders under the legal process.

Additional security

Any other security which may be taken by the lenders will not reduce the amount of the guarantee.

Representations and warranties

The borrower and each of the guarantors make the following representations and warranties to the lenders.

Status

It is a properly incorporated company and has the power to own its assets and carry on its business in its place of incorporation.

Power and authority

It has the power and authority to execute and perform its obligations under the finance documents and has taken all necessary corporate actions to do so.

Execution and delivery

The execution of the finance documents does not contravene any law or regulation to which it is subject, result in a breach or potential breach of any other obligation it has, contravene the provisions of its Memorandum and Articles of Association or other constitutional documents, result in any limit of its borrowing powers being exceeded, or create any adverse effect on its undertaking and assets (i.e. its market reputation).

Pari passu

Its obligations under the finance documents are direct and unconditional and rank at least pari passu with its other indebtedness (any allowed exceptions will be stated).

No proceedings

No legal proceedings are in course or threatened against the borrower or any guarantor which could have a material adverse effect on the repayment of the loan. If the borrower operates in an industry where it could well have minor claims regularly made against it, it may insist on a maximum amount of such claims being allowed and stated here.

No default

Nothing which is or could become an event of default under the loan agreement has occurred, either under these finance documents or any other facilities from other lenders.

No encumbrance

No security has been given to any other lender, and there is no obligation to give any. If any has been given, it is shown here as a permitted encumbrance.

Financial information

The latest consolidated accounts of the obligor were prepared under GAAP and give a true and fair view of the financial condition of the obligor, and since the date of those accounts there has been no material adverse change in the obligor's financial condition.

No misleading information

The information contained in the information memorandum was true and accurate, any financial projections given were prepared on reasonable assumptions, and nothing was omitted or withheld or has since occurred which would make the information memorandum misleading.

Repetition

All the representations and warranties are deemed to be repeated, and are thus deemed still to be in place, at the date of each drawdown request and the first day of each interest period.

Undertakings

The loan agreement states that each of the following undertakings given by the borrower and the guarantors shall remain in force from the date of signature of the loan agreement until the loan is fully repaid.

Financial statements

The borrower and the guarantors will supply copies of their audited consolidated annual accounts as soon as they are available, and in any event within a stated number of days: typically 120 days from their financial year ends. They will also supply copies of their unaudited consolidated interim accounts within a stated number of days. These copies will be supplied to the agent in a sufficient number of copies that the agent will deliver one to each of the lenders. Occasionally the loan agreement will call for more frequent management accounts to be delivered, such as on a quarterly or monthly basis.

Other information

The borrower undertakes to supply the agent with copies of all press releases or statements made to its shareholders or creditors; to advise the agent of any litigation which could have a material adverse effect on the loan; and to supply the agent with any other financial information which the agent may reasonably request. In practice, the agent would only call for this further information if the loan had started to show problems.

Change of business and disposals

The borrower undertakes that, without the prior written consent of the agent, no substantial change in the nature of its business will be made, no merger or corporate reconstruction will be made, and no material assets will be sold or disposed of. This disposal sub-clause may contain a wording such as other than in the normal course of its business or trading or other than disposals of assets in exchange for other assets of a comparable type or value or where those assets exceed 5% of the total consolidated assets of the group, as the lenders obviously do not wish to prevent the borrower from carrying out its normal business. The borrower also undertakes to keep all insurances current and to comply with the terms of any consent it has received in relation to the loan.

Notification of default

The borrower undertakes to notify the agent of any occurrence which might affect its ability to perform its obligations under the loan agreement or lead to a potential event of default as soon as it becomes aware of it, together with any steps it is taking to rectify the position. It will, if required by the agent, deliver to the agent a certificate stating that no event of default or potential event of default has occurred.

Financial covenants

As with all the terms and conditions of a syndicated loan facility, the financial covenants given by the borrower will vary from case to case. They should not be drawn so tightly that the borrower finds it difficult to carry out its normal business, and some scope will normally be given for slight downturns. Indeed, on some occasions none are stated, or one or two general conditions may be included such as a provision that consolidated net worth must not be lower at the end of one financial year than it was at the end of the previous year, and/or a restraint on dividends being paid. However, there will generally be a list of financial covenants to which the borrower must adhere, not least because any breach or near breach can give an early warning signal to the lenders that all is not going well and action may have to be contemplated to protect the lenders' position.

Some of the most usual financial conditions are shown here. They will be given by both the borrower and any guarantors, although some of the figures or ratios may differ. Each of the capitalized terms will be defined in the definitions clause or at the end of this clause, and all calculations must be made in accordance with GAAP:

- *Net worth*: Consolidated tangible net worth shall not be less than GBP x.
- *Debt/equity*: Total liabilities shall not exceed x per cent of net worth.

- *Gearing*: Net borrowings shall not exceed x per cent of net worth.
- *Current ratio*: Current liabilities shall not exceed x per cent of current assets.
- *Interest cover and tax*: Interest costs shall not exceed x per cent of earnings before interest.
- *Receivable cover*: The aggregate of all financial indebtedness, excluding intra group indebtedness, shall not exceed x per cent of eligible debtors. All financial indebtedness may be replaced by indebtedness under this loan facility, and any other specified facilities.
- *Cash flow*: In respect of each financial period, available cash flow shall not be less than GBP x. (This is a comparatively brief and simple example of cash flow, which has become increasingly important to lending bankers, and so this sub-clause may be considerably expanded.)
- *Working capital*: Working capital shall not be less than GBP x.
- *Restriction on distributions*: The borrower may not, without the prior written consent of the lenders, pay any dividends or repurchase its own shares if the available cash flow does not cover such payment by a factor of x, and/or if the amount of the payment would exceed x per cent of the net profits for the same period, and/or if there has been an event of default.
- *Restrictions on capital spending*: The borrower shall not incur capital expenditure in an aggregate amount exceeding GBP x. This shall include expenditure in respect of the acquisition of another business, unless the consideration is satisfied by the issue or allotment of shares. The lenders may agree to certain exclusions, and indeed the purpose of the loan may be to make just such an expenditure, and any such exclusions will be stated here.

Compliance certificate

The borrower undertakes to supply to the agent on stated dates (normally quarterly throughout the life of the loan) compliance certificates setting out in reasonable detail its computations to show that the financial covenants are being adhered to. The compliance certificate will be signed by two directors of the borrower, and sometimes by its auditors.

Negative pledge

This sub-clause states that the borrower may not give security to other lenders to it, or allow any security it has already given to remain in place unless the lenders agree to this, in which case it will be known as a permitted encumbrance and noted here. It may not enter into any sale and lease back arrangement or dispose of or sell its receivables on a with recourse basis (possibly with the exception of bills of exchange which are sold with recourse in the ordinary course of its business).

If the borrower makes an acquisition of another company which has already given security to another lender, this is permitted so long as it does not increase, and it is cancelled within a stated period (usually 3 months) or, if this cancellation is not allowed under the existing documentation, the underlying indebtedness is repaid in accordance with the repayment schedule.

Events of default

Events of default are occurrences under which the agent may, if instructed so to do by a majority group of lenders, accelerate the loan and call for immediate repayment. They apply to the borrower and its subsidiaries and all guarantors, and may include the following:

- *Non-payment*: If any amount due is not paid on the due date in the correct currency, or within a specified number of days thereafter if the non-payment is for technical reasons.
- *Financial covenants*: If any of the financial covenants are broken.
- *Other obligations*: If any other obligation is broken, e.g. if the borrower falls into default in another loan. A period of time may be stated in which the borrower may make good the breach unless the agent has the reasonable opinion that the breach is not capable of being remedied.
- *Misrepresentation*: If any representation or statement made in any of the finance documents, including the information memorandum, proves to be wrong or misleading.

- *Cross default*: If any indebtedness of the borrower or a guarantor is not paid when due, or becomes payable earlier than originally scheduled because of an event of default in that loan, or if any guarantee or indemnity is called. Some borrowers who have a range of loan facilities from different lenders are able to mitigate this sub-clause somewhat by negotiating that the amount involved to trigger a cross default must be higher than a stated amount.
- *Insolvency*: If a receiver or administrator is appointed over the borrower or a guarantor or it becomes insolvent, or if any act of insolvency or insolvency proceedings occurs.
- *Change*: If the borrower or a guarantor ceases to carry on the whole or a substantial part of its business, or is acquired by another company.
- *Unlawfulness*: If it should become unlawful for the borrower or a guarantor to perform its obligations under the finance documents. This sub-clause may appear odd; what is the point of the lenders declaring an event of default and calling for repayment if the borrower is prevented from repaying by law? However, it may be that the new law applies to the borrower but not the guarantor (or vice versa), or perhaps the borrower or guarantor will have assets overseas and could be sued for repayment in a different jurisdiction.
- *Conditions Precedent*: If any of the Conditions Precedent ceases to be correct, or if any material consent is withdrawn or revoked.
- *Repudiation*: If any of the finance documents is repudiated by the borrower or a guarantor or it becomes invalid.
- *Material adverse change*: If any event occurs which, in the opinion of the lenders, may jeopardize the due repayment of the loan. Some borrowers will not agree to the inclusion of this sub-clause, or will insist upon it being more tightly drawn, on the grounds that it gives too wide a scope for the lenders to call for repayment.

Indemnities

The borrower indemnifies the agent and the lenders against any loss or expense (including loss of profit) they may suffer as a result of any default by the borrower, the consequences of an event of default, interest break costs due to early repayments, and a drawdown not being made for any reason after a drawdown notice has been received.

Currency

This clause sets out the way in which the agent will convert one currency to another if a repayment is for any reason made in the wrong currency. The borrower indemnifies the agent and the lenders against any loss they may suffer through this conversion, but the agent agrees to reimburse the borrower with the amount of any surplus which may arise.

The agent and lenders

Once the loan agreement is signed, the arranger plays no further part unless, as is common, it is also acting as agent.

The agent is appointed irrevocably by the lenders, who authorize it to exercise the provisions of the loan agreement and any other finance documents such as security documents.

The agent's duties are purely administrative and it has no obligations to any party other than those stated in the loan agreement. In carrying out its duties it may rely upon any information it believes to be genuine, and it is entitled to believe that all documents are valid and appropriately authorized. It may appoint lawyers, accountants, and other experts and receives indemnities for their payment. It is bound to act in accordance with instructions it receives from the majority banks, or all the lenders in those circumstances for which the loan agreement requires unanimous agreement (though it need not do so until it receives an indemnity or other security it requires for its costs, or if it believes that the instructions would breach any law or regulation), and in the absence of such instructions it may act or refrain from acting in what it considers to be in the best interests of the lenders. It is not authorized to act on behalf of other lenders in any legal proceedings until it is authorized by that lender, but in a syndicated loan this authority is usually given. It is not responsible for the accuracy of any information given to the lenders or for the validity or completeness of the finance documents. The lenders confirm that they have made their own credit decisions without relying upon the agent. It is not liable for any action it is instructed to make except by gross negligence or wilful misconduct.

The agent may resign from its role, but this resignation will only take effect when a new agent is appointed. The new appointment can be made within

30 days by the majority banks, or, failing that, the original agent may itself appoint the new agent. The resigning agent must deliver all records and documents relating to the loan to the new agent, and it will then be discharged from any further obligations connected with the loan facility.

An agent may be removed by the majority banks, who must then appoint a successor within 30 days.

Sharing payments

This clause deals with payments which may be wrongly received direct from the borrower by a lender, instead of through the agent. The effect is that the lender must pay the funds to the agent for distribution amongst all the lenders.

The clause can also be used to cover situations such as a war or dispute breaking out between the countries of origin of the borrower and one of the lenders, where the borrower is made by law or regulation to reduce a payment by the amount due to that lender. In those circumstances the agent will pay all the lenders pro rata, and claim the amount of the underpayment from the borrower.

Transfers of participations

During the life of a syndicated loan, the lenders are free (subject to certain conditions) to sell their participations in the loan to other banks. There are four main ways in which this may be accomplished:

- by risk participation,
- by sub-participation,
- by assignment,
- by novation.

Here, we will concentrate on transfers by way of novation as the draft documentation to effect a transfer by way of novation is normally contained in the loan agreement.

Novation involves the extinguishing of the rights and obligations of the seller and the creation of identical new rights and obligations by the buyer, as if a completely new loan is being made.

Conditions of transfer

The consent of the borrower is normally required, unless the transfer is to be made to an existing lender or an affiliate of a lender. The loan agreement usually states that this consent shall not be unreasonably withheld or delayed, and if the borrower has not responded within five business days, it will be deemed to have given its consent.

Some loans are syndicated on the basis of a minimum participation being held by each lender, and if a transfer would result in the original lender or the new lender holding less than this minimum, consent may not be given. Transfers may also only be permitted in multiples of, for example, 1 million pounds.

Transfer fee

The new lender must pay a fee, stated here, to the agent to cover its costs as the work involved is not covered by the annual agency fee which the agent receives from the borrower.

Responsibility of lenders

The selling lender takes no responsibility for the finance documents, the financial condition of the borrower or the guarantors, their performance of the terms and conditions of the loan, or the accuracy of the information memorandum or any other information given.

The buying lender confirms that it has made its own investigation into the creditworthiness of the loan and is not relying upon any information given to it by the selling lender.

The selling lender is under no obligation to take back the transferred participation or make good any losses of the buying lender in the event of a default or similar breach of the terms and conditions of the loan.

Procedure for transfer

A form of transfer certificate will be set out as a schedule to the loan agreement. An example would be as follows:

Form of Transfer Certificates

To: as agent
From: (the existing lender) and
 (the new lender)
Date:
Megaco UK plc

GBP 150,000,000 term loan agreement dated (the loan agreement)
1 We refer to clause (procedure for transfer) of the loan agreement.
  (a) The existing lender and the new lender agree to the existing lender and the new lender transferring by novation all or part of the existing lender's commitment, rights and obligations referred to in the schedule in accordance with clause .... (Procedure for Transfer).
  (b) The proposed transfer date is ....
  (c) The facility office and address, fax number and attention details for notices of the new lender for the purposes of clause (Addresses) are set out in the schedule.
2 The new lender expressly acknowledges the limitations on the existing lender's obligations set out in paragraph x of clause (limitation of responsibility of existing lenders).
3 This transfer certificate is governed by English Law.

The schedule
Commitment/rights and obligations to be transferred (amount and any other relevant details such as whether this is the whole of the existing bank's participation or only a part).

	Existing lender	New lender
Name:		
Facility office address:		
Fax number:		
Attention detail for notices:		
Account details:	for and on behalf of ABC Bank plc	for and on behalf of XYZ Bank plc

This Transfer Certificate is accepted by the agent and the Transfer Date is confirmed as ....

Wolfsbane Trowektool III
for and on behalf of agent Bank plc

The selling lender will produce and sign the transfer certificate and forward it to the buying lender, who signs it and forwards it to the agent for execution once the agent has received the consent of the borrower. From the transfer date, all parties to the loan have the same rights and obligations with the new lender as they had with the previous one.

NB: The choice of the transfer date can be important to the selling lender if it has match funded the loan, as it may suffer a break-finding cost as a result of receiving funds early. Similarly, the new lender may find that because the cost of funding has risen since the interest rate was last set, he will not be receiving the full interest margin. If the end of an interest period is imminent, the transfer date may therefore be matched to the end of the interest period.

Disclosure. Under this sub-clause, an existing lender proposing to transfer its participation is enabled to disclose information concerning the loan and the obligors to potential new lenders. Without this sub-clause, this could be a breach of the duty of confidentiality between banker and customer.

Changes to the obligors

The obligors are precluded from transferring any of their rights and obligations. The borrower may propose that a wholly owned subsidiary becomes an additional or alternate borrower, which needs the unanimous consent of all the lenders. The same unanimous consent would be required for any changes to the guarantors. At the date of becoming an additional obligor, that company would be deemed to be complying with all the applicable representations set out in the loan agreement.

Notices. This clause states that all notices from one party to another must be given in writing, to the addresses given in the loan agreement unless a change is subsequently notified. They may be given by letter, fax, or telex (not, at the time of writing, by E-mail, although this is beginning to be seen). If made by letter, the notice will be deemed to have been delivered at the time of delivery if delivered by hand or, for example, 2 days after the date of dispatch if sent by first class mail. If made by fax or telex, it will be at the time of sending provided that the correct answerback or equivalent is received. These times refer to working hours during working days, otherwise the time is carried forward to the next working day, and the notices must be marked for the attention of the department or person specified in the loan agreement. They must be in English or which other language is specified.

Waivers, amendments, and consents

This clause states that if the agent decides not to take any action or remedy available to it, this does not act as a waiver; the right to take action subsequently is retained. Similarly, if the agent has a number of options open but acts on only one, it retains the right to act under the others subsequently.

The agent may, if instructed so to do by the lenders, grant waivers over or consents to changes to the terms and conditions of the loan agreement. This may be authorized by the lenders under the majority lenders basis unless unanimous approval is required. This is usually in the cases of:

- Any extension to a payment date.
- Any reduction in payments to be made by the borrower.
- Any reduction in the interest rate or any fees or commissions payable by the borrower (this does not include the agency fee payable to the agent as this is not included in the loan agreement).
- Any increase to the amount of the facility.
- Any change to the borrower or guarantors.

Partial invalidity

If any provision of any of the finance documents becomes invalid or illegal, the other provisions are not affected. The effect of this clause can be, for example, that if the borrower is barred by statute or regulation from repaying the loan, a guarantor in another jurisdiction cannot claim that its guarantee has become invalid.

Governing law and jurisdiction

This clause determines the legal jurisdiction of the loan. For our purposes we will presume that this is English.

The loan agreement is stated to be governed by and construed in accordance with English law, and each of the parties irrevocably agrees that the English courts shall have jurisdiction to hear and determine any suit brought before them. However, it does not rule out the lenders taking action in any other jurisdiction, or both, if they so chose.

If the borrower is domiciled overseas, it must appoint a process agent in England to accept service of legal proceedings on its behalf. This means that, in the event of a default, the agent may serve notice of legal proceedings on the process agent and this will count as though the notice has been served on the borrower itself (even if the process agent neglects to advise the borrower that it has received this notice). The process agent will commonly be either a firm of solicitors or the Law Debenture Society.

Legal opinions

The loan agreement will require that a legal opinion is given by the lawyers acting on behalf of the lenders that the loan facility will be legally enforceable in all respects. If the borrower is domiciled overseas, there will also be a requirement for another legal opinion to be given by a firm of solicitors in that country stating that the loan agreement is enforceable under local laws and regulations, and covering such considerations as whether withholding tax or foreign exchange restrictions are currently applicable. There may also be a requirement for the borrower's solicitors to confirm that the borrower is a validly constituted company, that the terms and conditions of the loan agreement do not breach any of the constitutional documents of the borrower and that, when signed, the loan agreement will be a properly authorized debt of the borrower. Until the loan agreement is signed, these legal opinions will exist in draft form only in case of any last minute changes in local laws and regulations, and so one of the conditions precedent is that the legal opinions will be received in the form agreed in draft by the lenders before the loan may be drawn. It is the agent's responsibility to ensure that they are received and that the lenders are informed. The text of the draft legal opinions will appear as a schedule to the loan agreement.

The legal opinions will contain disclaimers that have to be judged by potential lenders individually. The reputation of the legal firms giving the opinion, and the amount of insurance they carry or are likely to carry against negligence, should also be assessed as far as this is possible.

The legal opinions to be given by the overseas lawyers will vary widely, but the text of the opinion given by the English legal advisers acting on behalf of the lenders will typically read as follows (see box on page 123).

The setting out of the terms and conditions applying to the loan, and the rights and responsibilities of the various parties, is now complete. It will now be signed by all parties, in sufficient number of copies that each party has one signed original, at a signing ceremony. Later, the agent will distribute other conformed copies (i.e. with the names of the various signatories but not their signatures) to the lenders for their working records. The names and addresses of all the participating banks will be set out in a schedule to the loan agreement which also shows their individual commitment.

Now the agent will ensure that the conditions precedent are fulfilled and, once they are, the loan can be drawn.

Sample legal opinion

Date ....
To: Agent Bank plc and the banks herein referred to

Dear Sirs,

We have acted as your legal advisers in England in connection with an agreement (the Loan Agreement) dated between (the Borrower), a company domiciled in ...., certain banks referred to therein (the banks), and yourselves as agent. We have taken instructions solely from the agent in connection with the preparation of the Loan Agreement. In this connection we refer to the following documents:

1 The Loan Agreement
2 The guarantee of ....
3 The Form of Opinion set forth in the 'Schedule to the Loan Agreement'.

This opinion is confined to and given on the basis of English law currently applied by the English courts. We have made no independent investigation of the laws of (country of domicile of the borrower) as a basis for this opinion and do not express or imply any opinion thereon but rely, to the extent that such laws affect this opinion, on the opinions referred to in clause .... of the loan agreement. We have assumed that there is nothing in the law of any other place which affects this opinion. This opinion is given on the basis that it will be governed by and construed in accordance with English law.

In giving this opinion we have assumed in relation to the Loan Agreement that (a) all the signatures on the originals of the Loan Agreement are genuine, (b) the execution of the Loan Agreement is within the capacity and powers of and has recently been authorized, executed, and delivered by the parties thereto, and is binding on the parties thereto (other than the borrower).

Based upon the foregoing we are of the opinion that, so far as the laws of England are concerned and subject to the qualifications and reservations set out below, the Loan Agreement constitutes valid and legally binding obligations of the borrower.

Further, we are of the opinion that no stamp, registration or other similar taxes or charges are payable in the United Kingdom in respect of the execution or delivery of the Loan Agreement.

Although the opinion expressed above is limited to the valid and binding nature of the obligations of the borrower, the qualifications and reservations to which this opinion is subject are as follows:

1 Clause of the Loan Agreement provides for interest to be paid on overdue amounts. Such interest may amount to a penalty under English law and may therefore not be recoverable.
2 We express no opinion as to the enforceability of clauses of the Loan Agreement as we are not aware of such a provision being considered by the English courts, but in this connection it should be noted that a study of recent English judgements and legislation lead us to believe that contrary to previous practice an English court would now give judgement for a monetary amount, due in a currency other than sterling, in such other currency.
3 There could be circumstances in which an English court would not treat as conclusive those certificates and determinations which the Loan Agreement states are to be so treated.
4 Enforcement may be limited by general principles of equity; in particular nothing in this opinion is to be taken as indicating that the remedy of an order for specific performance of the issue of an injunction would be available in an English court in respect of the obligations arising under the Loan Agreement in that such remedies are available only at the discretion of the court. Specific performance is not usually issued where damages would be an adequate alternative.
5 The obligations of the borrower are subject to all laws affecting creditors' rights generally.

This opinion is given for the sole benefit of the agent and the banks which are the original parties to the Loan Agreement.

Yours faithfully,

Wolfsbane Troweltool III
Legal Council to the Banks

Chapter 7

Loan covenants

The function of loan covenants

Covenants are undertakings given by a borrower as part of a term loan agreement. Their purpose is to help the lender ensure that the risk attached to the loan does not unexpectedly deteriorate prior to maturity. Covenants may, for example, place restrictions on merger activity or on gearing levels. Breach of a covenant normally constitutes an event of default and, as a result, the loan may become repayable upon demand.

From the borrower's point of view covenants often appear to be an obstacle at the time of negotiating a loan and a burdensome restriction during its term. As mentioned, they may also precipitate default. In order to negotiate an appropriate set of covenants, however, it is important for the borrower to have an understanding of the logic underlying the lender's position.

In the first instance the lender is using covenants to protect itself against possible actions the borrower could take, especially in times of financial distress, which would damage the lender's position. These actions are looked at in more detail below. Taking this a stage further, however, it can be expected that if the lender is unable to achieve adequate protection via covenants it will seek compensation, for example by requiring a higher margin. In some instances the covenants ideally wanted by the lender may be unduly restrictive and it may therefore be cost-effective for the borrower to be prepared to pay more for a greater degree of freedom. In other cases, however, it will be possible to negotiate an economically acceptable set of covenants in return for more favourable terms elsewhere in the contract. In instances such as these, debt covenants can be of benefit to both lender and borrower.

The games borrowers play

What specific actions by borrowers are lenders seeking to protect themselves against? These can be classified as financing, dividend or investment decisions that it is feared borrowers may take to enhance their own financial position at the expense of that of the lenders.

Financing decisions

The borrower could dilute the claim of the lender in question by subsequently raising additional debt having an equal or even a prior claim over the company's assets. If the original lender did not allow for this eventuality, then the borrower will have gained at the expense of the lender's position having become more risky.

Dividend decisions

A loan may be extended in the expectation that the borrower will maintain existing dividend and reinvestment policies. However, the borrower may start to pay out dividends in excess of those envisaged by the lender at the expense of capital spending, so reducing the lender's asset backing.

Investment decisions

Two contrasting problems are anticipated under this heading: a failure to undertake certain potentially profitable investments and an over-eagerness to embark on excessively risky ones.

Under investment

Take the example of a company in financial distress, i.e. one whose outstanding loans exceed its asset value. The shareholders of such a company may be unwilling to finance a profitable project if they perceive that most of the benefit will simply accrue to the creditors by way of reducing the shortfall in asset value. In effect this is the dividend payment problem under another guise. Excessive dividends entail an unexpected cash outflow whereas here shareholders are failing to inject funds into the business.

Increasing business risk

Continuing with the example of a financially distressed company, it could be advantageous to the shareholders to switch into investments or business projects that are riskier than those that were held at the time the original loan was made. This is because in the likely event that such a project will fail, given its high risk, the loss will be borne in the main by the company's creditors in the form of an even lower payout than they were going to receive in the first place. In the improbable event of a substantial profit, however, the bulk of the benefit will accrue to the shareholders because the creditors' claims cannot exceed a fixed amount. Given the originally shaky position of the company, an increase in business risk will thus benefit the shareholders and disadvantage the creditors.

In summary then, lenders negotiating term loans will be concerned that, once the facility is in place, borrowers may unexpectedly raise additional debt finance with an equal or prior claim; pay out excessive dividends; fail adequately to maintain asset levels; or increase the risk profile of the company's assets. These would all be ways of benefiting the borrower at the expense of the lender. Moreover they are particularly relevant in the context of financially troubled companies. This is for two reasons. First, the raising of excessive amounts of additional debt can itself hasten financial distress. Second, the dividend and investment policies described are most likely to benefit shareholders at the expense of lenders when the company is already in or approaching financial difficulties.

Functions of loan covenants

In light of the above it would appear that loan covenants have four key functions:

- To place some restraint on the danger that a company may become financially distressed. This is achieved, e.g. by gearing limits.

- To provide the banker with an early warning if, nevertheless, a company is beginning to have problems or is significantly changing the nature of its operations.
- To limit the extent to which borrowers can take actions such as those described above, which they may be particularly tempted to do when approaching financial distress.
- Finally, if necessary, to trigger loan default.

Proponents of the use of covenants, emphasizing the early warning function of covenants, take the case further by arguing that well-designed covenants provide not only timely performance indicators but also open up lines of communication between borrower and lender. Thus 'covenants provide the borrower with certainty as to what may cause the bank to become concerned ... (and) in difficult times, when the company may need the forbearance and possibly active support of its banks, covenants ensure that the banks feel well informed, supportive and less likely to impede a hard pressed management or to panic and accelerate unnecessarily'.

Drawbacks to loan covenants

It is, nevertheless, recognized that covenants are not a universal panacea for resolving lender–borrower conflicts. For example at some time during the term of a loan a once-relevant covenant may require amendment due to a change in circumstances. However, this may be costly to achieve, especially where a company has many bilateral agreements all requiring amendment or a syndicated facility requiring a large majority, or even unanimity, to agree amendments. Also, contractual restrictions on management activity can turn out to be more costly than the damage they are intended to limit. This is partly because covenants are sometimes a very blunt tool for controlling certain management activities, in particular investment decisions. Furthermore setting appropriate levels for ratio covenants is not a science. If the ratios are too loose they will fail to control for the matters discussed above. If they are too tight, they will place unnecessary restrictions on the borrower and may trigger an unwarranted default.

Guidelines for efficient covenanting

It is this recognition of both the costs and benefits of covenants that has led one writer to suggest three guidelines for efficient covenanting:

- Covenants place limitations on borrower action. Therefore, in return, they must be seen to provide lenders with an appropriate form of economic protection. For example, to what extent does the widely used borrowings/capital and reserves ratio, based as it is on balance sheet values, actually provide the lender with either a measure of asset backing or a reliable indicator of impending financial distress?
- Covenants should not be so extensive that the protection afforded to the lender is outweighed by the costs they impose on the borrower in terms of restrictions on management action. For example, it would be very difficult to design a covenant that would directly protect the lender from the under-investment problem described above. This is because it would be impossibly intrusive to monitor a company's failure to undertake particular investments. Instead it usually suffices to track investment policy indirectly, for example via minimum net worth or current ratio covenants.
- For any desired degree of lender protection the least restrictive covenant should be used.

The above points focus on the costs and benefits of covenanting. While it may not be possible to quantify these costs and benefits, it is suggested that they are useful guidelines to bear in mind when negotiating a contract.

Types of covenants

This section reviews the main covenants usually found in UK bank loan agreements. It covers non-financial and financial covenants as well as events of default, which can be triggered by covenant violations. It concludes by summarizing the economic functions of the various covenants. This also indicates potential duplication of effort and unnecessary restriction of borrower activity when more than one covenant performing a similar function is included in a contract.

Non-financial covenants

Four important non-financial covenants are as follows:

- *Negative pledge*. This prevents the borrower from giving some future lender prior security over its assets.
- Guarantees provided by members of a group of companies for the debt of other members of that group.
- An undertaking to supply the lender with periodical financial information. Over and above the annual audited accounts, management accounts are the most frequently required, often on a quarterly basis.
- Restrictions on capital spending, acquisitions and asset disposals.

Financial covenants

The most common financial covenants used in UK bank lending stipulate minimum net worth, interest cover and gearing (ratio of borrowings to net worth). Current ratio, cash flow ratio (e.g. cash flow interest cover) and asset disposal/net worth covenants are also used although less frequently. By way of contrast, gearing and asset disposal/asset covenants tend to predominate in UK bond and debenture issues, whereas direct dividend restrictions are common in US private lending agreements.

Events of default

Events of default are those events, which, should they occur, permit the lender to require all amounts outstanding to become immediately payable. The typical events of default clauses are as follows:

- Failure to pay amounts owing to the lender when due.
- Failure by the borrower to perform other obligations under the loan agreement. It is due to this clause that a covenant violation triggers an event of default.
- Any representation or warranty made by the borrower proving to be untrue.
- Cross-default, i.e. where the borrower has triggered an event of default or has actually been put into default on any other loan agreement.

- Where a 'material adverse change' has occurred in the borrower's financial or operating position. This is clearly a 'catch-all' clause and there is a view that 'where a company has negotiated a meaningful set of covenants, it can legitimately refuse to accept a continuing material adverse change clause'.

Objectives of individual covenants

A clear understanding of what individual covenants are aiming to achieve can help the borrower avoid unnecessary duplication. As the following listing of objectives shows, any one covenant can meet multiple aims:

- To restrict excessive debt, accomplished by:
  - gearing covenant, due to the widespread use of tangible net worth in this ratio, it works particularly against debt-financed acquisitions of goodwill and other intangibles;
  - interest cover;
  - current ratio, which guards against funding fixed asset expansion with short-term debt.
- To protect the lender's priority vis-à-vis other creditors, achieved by:
  - negative pledge;
- To prevent excessive dividend payouts:
  - minimum net worth achieves this by safeguarding the level of reserves;
  - current ratio, which safeguards liquid asset levels out of which dividends have to be paid;
  - gearing addresses both reserves and liquid assets;
  - specific dividend pay-out restraints may be imposed to cover future 'super' profits.
- To trigger loan default if profits fall below expectation:
  - interest cover warns against shortfalls in the current year's operating profits;
  - minimum net worth signals insufficient cumulative retained profits;
  - gearing also signals low cumulative profits via inclusion of net worth in the ratio.

- To prevent changes in the borrower's business risk profile:
  - restrictions on capital spending and acquisition levels can achieve this only indirectly.

In practice it is quite common for a contract to contain two of the three most standard financial covenants (net worth, interest cover and gearing) and not unusual for all three to be present. The above analysis suggests, however, that a minimum net worth covenant may not be adding much to a contract, which already has gearing and interest cover covenants.

Negotiating the covenants in the loan agreement

Bankers use standardized documentation as the starting point for negotiating the various types of term loan they offer. This may be produced in-house or by one of the few London law firms specializing in work of this nature. There appears to be a fair amount of standardization throughout the market in these contract 'boiler-plates', which serves only to emphasize the importance of an appropriate negotiating strategy from the borrower's viewpoint.

Covenants are not legal technicalities

The corporate treasurer is usually responsible for negotiating loan terms. It is important that the treasurer should rely not only on legal advice, but also ensure that he or she is aware of the accounting technicalities and the likely range of projected values for key variables such as net worth and operating profit. Phrases such as 'the standard covenants shall apply' should be avoided, for they are likely to result in costly renegotiation at a later stage. As a City law firm partner has said: '... we are constantly requested to amend documents subsequently where borrowers have not realized the wide implications of a clause or the width of a defined term.'

Structured negotiations: understanding the lender's viewpoint

Arnold, an American banker, has set out a structured approach for borrowers entering such negotiations. In his view the lender will always require some form of reassurance about four key dimensions of the borrower's future performance, its financial structure, cash flows, asset levels and strategy. In addition the lender will want covenants to signal impending difficulties and, if necessary, to trigger default.

The nature of the reassurance and covenants that the lender will aim to achieve will depend on (a) the borrower's profitability and financial strength, and (b) the likely variability or risk underlying these. Companies can thus be seen as falling into one of four possible categories depending on their financial strength and business risk.

In the case of a borrower perceived as having a strong financial structure but a high level of business risk the lender may seek a gearing covenant aimed at preserving balance sheet strength; a tight minimum net worth covenant, closely tracking budgeted levels, to act as a sensitive trigger in case the downside risk results in large losses; and, anticipating that the high level of business risk may jeopardize refinancing as a source for loan repayment, various covenants have directed at limiting cash outflows, e.g. a capital spending limit.

For a large top-performing company ('low financial risk/low business risk'), on the other hand, the lender may be satisfied with a gearing covenant set well above forecast levels and a minimum net worth trigger, accompanied by an appropriate asset sale limitation.

A negotiating strategy for borrowers emerges from the above analysis. At the outset the borrower should evaluate its own strengths and weaknesses with a view to anticipating the lender's objectives and hence the covenants the lender would be justified in requiring. This will also involve an understanding of the economic function of the covenants usually demanded. In the light of this analysis each proposed covenant can then be discussed with a view to its exclusion or relaxation.

Economic rationale of the covenants 'package'

Research into covenant profiles finds that they do indeed vary according to the characteristics of the borrower, the loan and the economic environment. In other words there is, in general, an economic rationale underpinning the range or 'package' of covenants found in loan agreements. This covenants package can be examined under three headings: the number of covenants, how restrictive they are and the extent of tailoring of accounting definitions. The first two headings relate to all types of covenant, both financial and non-financial, whereas the third deals only with financial covenants.

Number of covenants

The following considerations are found to be associated with loan contracts containing a larger number of covenants. They are all factors that increase the riskiness of the proposition to the lender and/or place the borrower in a weaker negotiating position:

- the more highly geared the borrower; there is, however, a view that this can be taken too far, i.e. that 'banks often fail to insist on sound covenants while business is good; they then load sick companies with more than can really have value'.
- the larger the loan, measured, for example, relative to net tangible assets
- the smaller the borrowing company
- the absence of security
- the longer the term of the loan
- when the market demand for loans is strong relative to the supply. One observer has commented: 'perhaps the most convincing aid in negotiating less restrictive covenants is competition', although its efficacy will depend on the state of the lending market at any point in time.

According to these findings, features of a loan that increase its risk (e.g. absence of security) are compensated for by covenants. There may be propositions, however, that are so risky that the lender will require both security and covenants. Thus, while covenants are usually substitutes for other forms of lender protection, they may sometimes complement them. There are factors influencing new lenders to standardize their covenants with those in a borrower's existing loan agreements. This reduces both the borrower's reporting burden and the risk of unwanted cross-default from the lender's viewpoint.

The restrictions of covenants

There is evidence that ratio covenants tend to be tighter the higher the gearing, the larger the loan and smaller the borrower. These findings all follow the same logic as do the factors influencing the number of covenants. Interestingly there is one loan feature where the logic appears to reverse the term of the loan. While there is some evidence that longer-term loans are associated with more covenants, these covenants tend to be looser so as not to place undue restrictions on management action extending into the long-term future.

In practical terms the borrower should use financial statement projections to gauge the likelihood of violating ratio covenants, e.g. what fall in profits would depress shareholders' funds so much that a proposed gearing covenant would be breached? In the same vein, if covenants are tested more than annually, they should take account of seasonal dips in performance. Forecasts are probably used less in practice than they should be, however. This is either due to larger companies' reluctance to disclose such information, or the lack of budgets among smaller borrowers. In fact, forecasts can be used as a powerful aid to negotiation. For example, a UK banker describes a situation with a tight covenant and a dual pricing structure, with the margin and commitment fee being lower if reported results outperform the covenanted level by an agreed amount.

Clearly the concept of restrictions can also be applied to non-financial covenants. For example, there may be grace periods before defaults bite; defaults may apply only to 'material' subsidiaries; asset disposal restrictions may not apply if the majority of banks agree.

Tailoring accounting definitions

The definitions of the accounting items used in ratio covenants are heavily reliant on the numbers presented in the audited consolidated accounts. Often these figures are only the starting-point for a definition, however, so it is important for the borrower to understand the sorts of adjustments lenders are likely to include in a contract proposal.

There is evidence that accounting definitions are more likely to be adjusted the fewer the number of lenders being dealt with and the longer the term of the loan. This is because in such cases it is more cost-effective for the parties involved to negotiate definitions tailored to the particular needs of the case rather than to rely on Financial Reporting Standards (FRS), or Generally Accepted Accounting Principles (GAAP).

The aim of tailoring is to reduce the scope for conflict between lender and borrower, and this is achieved in two ways. One is to define items in a generally more objective and more conservative way than the FRS, or GAAP definition. The second is to take account of the specific circumstances of the borrower.

The objectivity and conservatism of the net worth figure used in minimum net worth and gearing covenants are often increased by excluding intangible assets and including only revaluation reserves based on independent valuations. Similarly the definition of borrowings widely includes guarantees for third-party indebtedness and other contingent liabilities. On the other hand the profit figure, which is included in the interest cover covenant and also makes its way into net worth, is rarely subject to a tight definition, possibly because it would be too costly to do so effectively.

Examples of tailoring definitions used in bank-loan contracts to specific circumstances are the exclusion of specified loans from borrowings or even their inclusion as part of net worth. Also the goodwill arising from a particular acquisition may be included in net worth, as may some brand values.

It is clearly important for the parties to loan negotiations to have a sound understanding of the accounting technicalities so that any unintended consequences can be avoided. While FRS and GAAP are widely used, for example, are these the principles in force at the time the contract was agreed ('frozen' FRS or GAAP) or those at the time of reporting to the bank ('rolling' FRS, or GAAP)? Rolling FRS, or GAAP seem to predominate in practice. While this approach is less costly to report, it can, however, result in covenants being violated simply due to changes in standard accounting procedures.

A wider issue related to accounting definitions, and indeed to the effectiveness of ratio covenants at all, is the question of how accurately a company's accounts reflect the underlying economic factors the covenants are supposedly controlling. Thus net balance sheet assets may be a relatively poor measure of the size of a company's asset base say, in the service sector where intangibles not appearing on the balance sheet are of the US that companies with a relatively large difference between share market capitalization and book value (used as a measure of the relevance of balance sheet assets) are less likely to have gearing covenants in their public debt issues. This section has shown that the covenant packages found in loan agreements follow an economic logic based on the characteristics of the loan, the parties to the loan (including negotiating power) and the market. The wide range of issues that can be subject to negotiation comprises the identity and number of covenants, how tightly they are set and the accounting definitions used.

Functioning of covenants during the loan

Monitoring compliance with covenants

If covenants are to be effective from the lender's viewpoint, periodical monitoring is clearly essential. There appears to be a discrepancy, however, between what is ideal for the lender and what can be achieved in practice. The frequent requirement that covenants should be complied with 'at all times' indicates that continuous compliance would best meet the banker's needs. In practice, however, the lender often has to make do with annual reporting, perhaps relying on a certificate of compliance from the directors. This may be because the customer is unwilling to supply accounts more frequently or because the bank lacks the resources to monitor more than once a year.

The restriction of management action by covenants

In the section 'The economic function of debt covenants' it was pointed out that, from the lender's viewpoint, one of the functions of covenants is to prevent a major increase in the risk of the loan. However, if the limitations imposed by the covenants are too restrictive, the benefit of the protection afforded to the lender will be outweighed by the cost of the restraints placed on normal management activity.

The value of the borrowing company may be impaired if, for example, its covenants place excessive restrictions on

- capital spending, which may mean the loss of profitable opportunities,
- asset disposals, which may reduce liquidity, or
- dividends, which may damage stock market standing.

Such covenants clearly influence management policy. The results of a US study of companies, which were close to violating their dividend covenant restrictions, showed a significant increase in the frequency of dividend cuts and omissions, continuing for several years.

There is, however, no systematic evidence quantifying the negative impact of these restrictions. The interesting US case of the Burlington Northern Railroad Company's (BNR) bond covenants indicates that such costs can be substantial. The covenants in question, which had been drawn up when the bonds were issued at the end of the nineteenth century, placed severe restrictions on BNR's use of the proceeds of property sales. In 1987 the bondholders agreed to the relaxation of these covenants in return for a payment of USD 35.5 million, equivalent to 30% of the face value of their bonds. The significant value of this settlement to BNR can be measured by the resulting 9.5% share price improvement (USD 475 million). As the case study concludes: 'when the loss to the shareholders became sufficiently large ... the firm was motivated to settle with the bondholders. Some of the increased value of the firm was redistributed in that process and some transaction costs were incurred. However, the value of the firm was increased by a relaxation of the covenant constraints'.

One reaction to the criticism that covenants can be unduly restrictive is that the pragmatic lending banker will generally agree to the modification of loan terms provided his risk is not affected. Thus a US banker wrote in the mid-1970s 'In any given year we will, on average, receive one modification request per loan on the books. In no more than about five per cent of these cases will we refuse the request or even require any quid pro quo, because the vast majority of corporate requests are perfectly reasonable and do not increase our risk materially'. However, this same writer does recognize that some lenders will be reluctant to agree to such modifications or may require a higher interest rate in return.

Accounting policies and adherence to financial covenants

Financial covenants often include lengthy accounting definitions to limit the extent to which choice of accounting methods can be used to avoid covenant breach. However, such definitions cannot prevent this happening altogether. In a survey of UK lending bankers, respondents were asked what action they would take if a customer made a disclosed accounting policy change, with the agreement of its auditors, boosting reported profit. In just under 60% of cases respondents indicated that they either could not or would not take any action. This means that in most cases the new accounting policy would be effective in moving the company away from its covenant limits.

To what extent do companies, which are close to covenant violation, adopt accounting policies in order to prevent a breach? There is a strong body of US-based empirical evidence that they do. Thus companies closer to certain covenant constraints have been found more likely to capitalize both interest and research and development expenditure.

Recognizing that it is unlikely that companies select individual accounting policies in isolation, a US study of a 'portfolio' of four accounting policies (stock valuation, depreciation, investment tax credit and pension cost amortization) finds an association between income-boosting accounting methods and closeness to covenant violation. A more recent US analysis, focusing on the same four accounting policies, compares companies that had violated financial covenants with those that had not. It finds that those in breach adopted significantly more profit-increasing accounting policies as early as 5 years prior to the breach.

The US literature makes a useful distinction between affirmative and negative covenants. The former include undertakings by the borrower to take specific actions and keep financial ratios within stated limits. Negative covenants proscribe certain investment and financing activities, such as dividend payments or asset disposals, unless specific financial measures are met. Companies may well adopt different approaches for avoiding the breach of these two types of covenant. The breach of a negative covenant is more likely to be avoided simply by refraining from the action proscribed by the covenant. This is illustrated in the study cited above of firms that were close to violating dividend restriction covenants. These firms showed no significant changes in accounting policies but instead cut back on dividend payments. By way of contrast, affirmative covenants such as gearing and net worth limits are far less easily controlled by operating policies. Therefore companies are more likely to resort to accounting policy changes to avoid breaching affirmative covenants.

Tightening up accounting definitions is not the only way of preventing borrowers using accounting policies in this way. A US study of companies engaged in significant amounts of leasing found that almost all of these companies' loan agreements omitted leases from the definitions of debt and assets used in financial covenants. This appeared on the face of it to open up the way for extended off-balance sheet activity. However, the agreements tended to prevent this by limiting activities such as sale and leaseback or additional rentals directly rather than via the accounting definitions.

Breach of covenant

Where breaches mostly occur

There is evidence from the US that covenant breaches almost always initially arise in private debt agreements. This is because the trust deeds of publicly held bonds are more costly to renegotiate due to the large number of parties involved. As a result their covenant limits are set more loosely than those in private debt contracts so as to reduce the risk of unintended violations.

In cases where financial covenants had been violated, the breach occurred in only one such covenant in as many as 45–60% of the instances. Three or more covenants were breached simultaneously in only 10–20% of cases. These findings suggest that there may not be a great deal of overlap between the functions of the various financial covenants.

The most frequently violated financial covenants in the US are tangible net worth (43% of violations studied); working capital or current ratio (29%); and gearing (19%). This shows that it is the breach of affirmative covenants that causes default. Negative covenants are rarely breached. Putting this in a UK context, while the three above-mentioned financial covenants are widely included in UK loan contracts, so is interest cover, which accounted for only 3% of violations in the US study.

The options open to the lending banker

A wide range of options is available to the lender when a customer is in breach of covenant. Starting with the most costly from the borrower's point of view, these are:

- recall the loan immediately;
- reserve rights to recall the loan at any time, i.e. convert it to being on demand;
- waiver following renegotiation;
- waiver for a limited time without renegotiation, in expectation of an improvement in the customer's position; and
- unconditional waiver without contract renegotiation.

The choice of which strategy is best is often a fine balancing act for the banker. '... Banks regard ratio covenants as deterrents, whose main function is to see that they are never needed … . On the other hand the knowledge that banks will use breaches of covenant to accelerate, if they have to, is vital if the whole exercise is to retain credibility'.

One way of looking at the banker's decision whether or not to accelerate is to view it as a trade-off decision between the bank's marketing and credit functions. Where a breach does not appear to reflect a serious threat to the customer's ability to repay, marketing considerations, in terms of an expected continued relationship with that customer, will have the upper hand. The more serious the borrower's underlying problems, the more likely are credit department requirements for repayment to prevail.

A US study of companies in breach of financial covenants corroborates these ideas. It finds that lenders are more likely to grant waivers, whether temporary or permanent, to companies with

- a lower estimated likelihood of eventually being wound up,
- lower gearing,
- secured loans,
- small loans.

Companies receiving temporary waivers had similar profiles to those receiving permanent waivers. Taking a different perspective, a survey of UK lending bankers finds that waivers are more likely where the customer informs the banker of an impending breach in advance. The likelihood of a waiver is increased further if the breach is caused by the goodwill arising from an acquisition rather than an underlying deterioration in financial health.

The cost to the borrower of breaching covenants

The costs of covenant violation can be categorized as follows:

- *Renegotiation costs*: the direct costs of renegotiation such as professional fees and management time.
- *Refinancing costs*: increased interest costs on the loan in question.
- *Restructuring costs*: the costs of refinancing or of modifying operating policies in order to meet lenders' repayment demands. For example, raising new debt will entail administrative costs and it may carry a higher interest rate. Also asset disposals may be required, although

the cost will depend on the profitability (or otherwise) of the discontinued operation.
- *Increased lender control*: new non-financial covenants tend to be imposed with a view to conserving the borrower's asset base, e.g. additional security, and dividend and capital spending restrictions.
- Existing financial covenants are often relaxed, but new financial covenants are rare.

Regarding renegotiation costs, a US study of companies filing for bankruptcy found that professional and administrative fees averaged 3.1% of company value. There is, however, no systematic evidence on the scale of these costs for companies that successfully restructure.

The renegotiation process

Due to its highly sensitive nature, there is no chronological data regarding the process of renegotiation. Confidentiality is virtually a prerequisite for success, especially if the borrower is a listed company. Compounding the problem is the high potential for conflict, not only between lender and borrower, but also among the often numerous lenders themselves. Both the Brent Walker and Berisford restructurings had to cope with more than 60 banks. The Bank of England's well-known London Approach guidelines encourage banks 'to contribute to an orderly management of crisis'. The success of the Berisford restructuring, for example, was due to a number of factors: the responsible behaviour of lenders and shareholders, the sale of the valuable British Sugar subsidiary, the identification of three separate lender groups and tailoring separate packages for each, and an early change in top management.

Other issues

This section examines three separate matters. It raises the question of how effective financial covenants are at signalling financial distress. It also discusses whether companies should be required to disclose information about their covenants. It concludes by looking at the impact of new accounting standards on compliance with financial covenants and the implications for accounting policy setters such as the Accounting Standards Board.

Financial covenants as predictors of financial distress.

One of the main functions of covenants is to provide the term lender with a timely signal of imminent financial difficulties. Are the measures most frequently used in financial covenants net worth, interest cover, gearing and the current ratio accurate indicators of financial distress?

There is no published research on the frequency with which financial covenants have enabled bankers to take timely action. Perhaps some indication is given by a US study of ratios as predictors of failure, which found that the four ratio categories that best distinguished between failed and non-failed companies in the year prior to failure were those measuring:

- rate of return, e.g. return on shareholders' funds;
- gearing;
- fixed payment coverage, e.g. interest cover;
- share price volatility.

Liquidity measures such as the current ratio did not perform well in the above sense. However, as pointed out in the section entitled 'Types of covenants', it must be remembered that covenants may have functions other than triggering potential default.

Disclosure of information about covenants

The primary objective of financial statement disclosure in both the UK and the US is to meet users' information needs. However, the two countries' disclosure requirements regarding debt contracts are very different.

In the UK, disclosure of bank loan covenants is virtually non-existent. The Combined Code of the Committee on Corporate Governance indicates that, if going concern uncertainties exist and the financial statements fail to disclose that covenants have been breached, then the audit report itself should make this disclosure. In a similar context a company close to a financial covenant limit may make a one-off disclosure.

In the US, by way of contrast, the Securities and Exchange Commission (SEC) requires a registrant to file 'all contracts, including indentures, involving debt issued in amounts, which exceed 10% of its total assets'. This includes both public and private debt agreements. Also Moody's Manuals provide summaries of public debt indentures. While US annual reports contain considerably more disclosure of financial covenants than those in the UK, the extent of this disclosure is inconsistent and usually not as complete as that available from Moody's or SEC filings. Whether covenant disclosure is desirable is an open question. Such information is likely to be relevant to users of financial statements. On the other hand there will be a fear that, in certain cases, disclosure itself may unnecessarily aggravate a company's financial difficulties.

Financial covenants and new accounting standards

Financial covenants are generally monitored using the accounting standards in force at the date of the financial statements under review. This means that a new accounting standard, unforeseen when the contract was drawn up, could put a company into default simply by changing the way in which the accounting numbers are calculated. Is a default such as this costly to borrowers?

The balance of evidence suggests that defaults caused by new accounting standards do not result in heavy costs for borrowers. In a survey of UK lending bankers, respondents were virtually unanimous in saying they would grant a waiver in such a situation. In one case in seven, however, they said they would use the breach as an opportunity for renegotiating other terms of the contract.

Furthermore, if lenders did react negatively to such breaches, it would be expected that the share prices of companies adversely affected by a proposed standard would suffer. The numerous US studies in this area indicate, on balance, no adverse share price impact, although this finding is not unanimous.

Chapter 8

Secondary loan markets

History and development of the secondary loan market (extracted from Loan Syndications and Trading Association (LSTA) web site, 2003)

The volume of secondary loan trading exploded in the 1990s. Between 1991 and 1999, volume grew over 1200%. In 1991, a total of USD 8 bn (face amount) of loans traded in the secondary market, according to Loan Pricing Corporation (LPC). In 1999, secondary volume grew to a total of USD 110 bn (face amount). This dramatic growth is shown in the chart on page 147.

There are many reasons why the secondary loan trading volume grew at an exponential rate. The syndicated new-issue loan market also grew over the same time period, although not as quickly. In 1999, the volume reached USD 1017 bn, according to LPC. This represents a 33.5% increase from 1991s total of USD 234 bn.

Additionally, during the early 1990s, default rates soared. Consequently, many banks felt the need to reduce their exposure to these distressed loans and sold them into a nascent secondary loan trading market. The chart shown above illustrates that volume of distressed loans in the secondary market was greater than par loan volume until 1994.

As a result of this growth in secondary loan trading volume, it became evident that uniform standards were needed for trading loans in the secondary market. The trading of loans is not subject to the same type of regulatory regime that governs securities. As a consequence, active market participants came together to develop market standards and principles.

Secondary loan markets

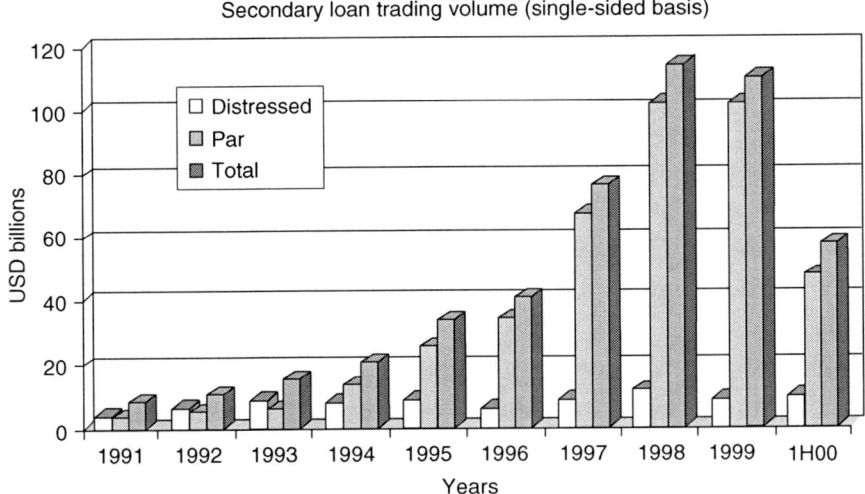

Source: LPC.

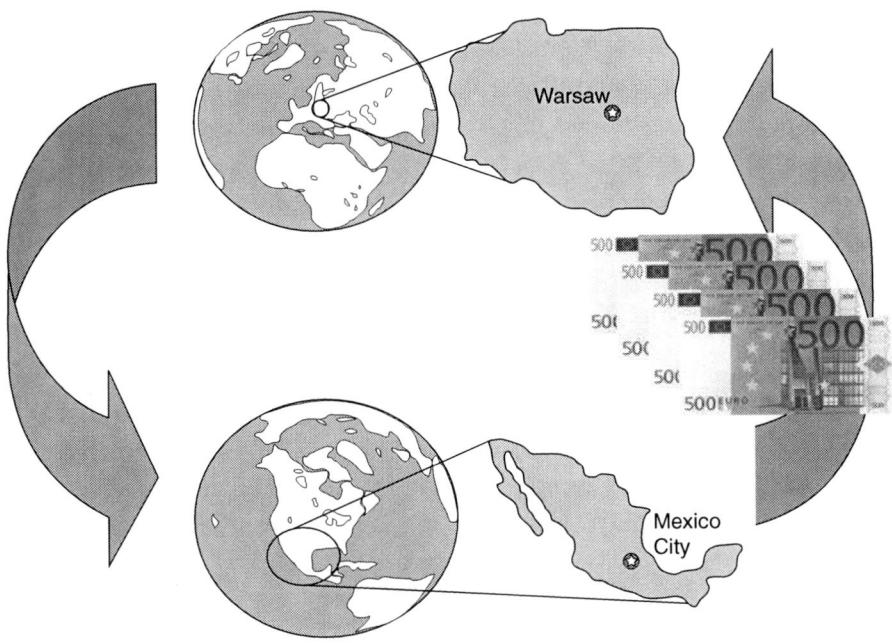

In December 1995 a group of loan traders pooled their resources in order to form an association in an effort to develop standard settlement and operational procedures, market practices and other mechanisms to trade the increasing volume of par and distressed bank debt more efficiently.

As a result, the Loan Syndications and Trading Association, Inc (LSTA) was formed.

The need and formation of the LSTA was not dissimilar to that of the International Swap Dealers Association, (ISDA), or the Emerging Markets Traders Association (EMTA). Prior to the formation of ISDA, swaps were cumbersome to trade and illiquid. Today, swaps are highly liquid and actively traded instruments.

In response to substantial growth in the European secondary loan market, several major financial institutions operating in Europe formed the Loan Market Association (LMA) in mid-1996. Headquartered in London, the LMA was established 'to create greater liquidity in the loan market through the development of a more active and efficient secondary market'. The LMA believes that increased standardization in both documentation and procedures will encourage timely settlement, reduce costs, and enable participants to exploit fully the secondary loan market. The LMA's initial agenda addresses information, valuation, settlement and operational procedures, and documentation for par assets only. However, the association fully expects to expand its focus in the future to include distressed loan assets.

Acknowledging the similar goals for their respective markets and the trend towards globalization of the US, European, and Asian loan markets, each of LMA and LSTA have agreed to keep each other informed of their progress towards a more efficient market. What is important to recognize is that the LMA has devised standards that are different than the LSTA. Therefore, it is essential to communicate with your counterparty as to which confirmation you are intending to use as it will affect the price of the loan.

Prior to the formation of the LSTA, many trade disputes occurred in the marketplace. The buyer of a loan had little certainty as to when settlement would occur. Counterparties would often argue about issues including who would receive a paydown on a loan between trade date and settlement date, which party would pay the assignment fee to the agent or how to allocate breakfunding costs. Today, as a result of the efforts of the LSTA to develop standard terms and conditions for loan trading, a buyer and a seller are not likely to end up in a trade dispute with each other.

LSTA

The Loan Syndications and Trading Association, Inc. (LSTA), founded in 1995, is a not-for-profit organization dedicated to promoting the orderly development of a fair, efficient, liquid, and professional trading market for corporate loans originated by commercial banks and other similar private debt.

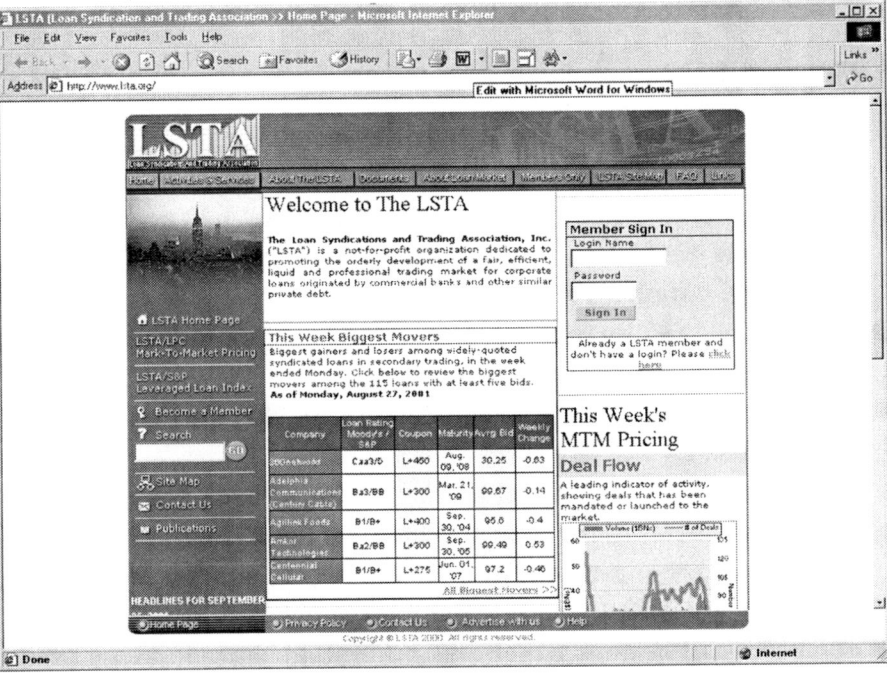

The LSTA consists of 41 full members, 24 associate members and 37 affiliate members. Founding Members are leading commercial banks and dealers, and institutions that have been and will continue to be instrumental in developing the association, its agenda and initiatives. Full members are institutions that directly or through affiliates, trade bank debt or invest in bank loans for their own account, such as dealers, commercial and investment banks, funds and insurance companies.

The affiliate member organizations have general interest in the market and include law firms, brokers, consultants, and advisers.

From an original membership of fifteen institutions, the LSTA has grown today to a total of 102 members. Members include commercial banks, investment banks, mutual funds, Collateralised Lease Obligation (CLO) fund managers, buy-side institutions, sell-side institutions, law firms, accounting firms, brokers, and many others.

The association's main goal is to promote the orderly development of a 'fair, efficient, liquid, and professional trading market for commercial loans and other similar private debt'. It is a not-for-profit association.

LSTA activities

The LSTA undertakes a variety of activities including:

- producing standard trading documentation for par and distressed loan assets (including standard confirmations, assignment agreements, and option agreement);
- establishing and publishing the LSTA/LPC Mark-to-Market Pricing Service (Loan Valuation);
- compiling and publishing, in agreement with S&P, the first third party return index for the leveraged loan market;
- publishing a code of conduct for the trading of bank debt;
- publishing weekly in the *Wall Street Journal* the 25 loans which experience the largest movement in price that week, number of loans that increased, decreased, and remained unchanged;
- organizing arbitration panel and arbitration procedures to resolve price disputes;
- establishing a forum for market participants to discuss important developments and relevant information.

Since its inception, the LSTA has adopted over 30 standardized documents, and has helped identify uniform market practices for use in the secondary loan market. The LSTA does not have legal authority to compel the use of its forms by market participants. The buyer and seller of a loan may choose to modify the recommended forms and closing procedures. However, it is recognized that the standards published by the LSTA have generally been accepted by the marketplace.

One of the most significant accomplishments of LSTA since its inception has been the establishment of standard settlement procedures, otherwise known as T + 10 for Par Loans (settlement date = trade date + 10 business days). This convention was formally introduced by LSTA in December 1995 and was quickly adopted by the loan trading marketplace.

LSTA committees

Most of the substantive work of the LSTA is achieved at the committee level. Members where they are able to identify the issues that are most important to them may attend the meetings of their choice. The committees are comprised of members of the business community who are most involved with the relevant issues. For example, the primary participants on the Distressed Debt Committee are distressed loan traders, distressed buy-side institutions, individuals involved in the workout departments of several banks, and law firms involved in distressed loan activities. Consequently, the work that comes out of the various committees fairly reflects the many different interests represented in the market:

- *Settlement committee* The settlement committee was formed to develop standardized documentation for trading par and near par loans and to address the issue of trades which do not settle on a timely basis. It was the settlement committee that developed and refined the form of confirmation for par/near par loans, which incorporates standard terms and conditions for such trades. It was also the settlement committee that developed close out procedures for failed trades and a funding memorandum (including delay compensation calculation). The committee has also adopted a standard multilateral letter agreement and a bilateral netting agreement. In addition to the above, the committee also reached consensus on standardizing the allocation of assignment fees in multiparty trades when it voted to have all parties involved in the trade split (per capita) the assignment fees.

- *Distressed debt committee* The distressed debt committee was formed in October 1996. Its goal was to address the issues relating to trading of distressed loan assets – bank debt, private notes and trade claims. This is one of the association's most active committees. As noted above, it has developed a number of significant documents for use in the distressed loan market: distressed trade confirmation together with standard terms and conditions; purchase and sale agreement for original assignments and secondary assignments for both borrowers in bankruptcy and not in bankruptcy, binding oral trade agreement; lost note affidavit and indemnity; confirmations and assignment agreement for trade claims; bid letter; and trade ticket. Finally, the committee regularly reports to its constituents on legal and regulatory developments that affect trading of distressed loan assets and credits.
- *Mark-to-market committee* The mark-to-market committee was formed to facilitate the collection of loan valuation information and the preparation of aggregate average statistics for monthly dissemination to assist in the accurate valuation of loan assets for financial reporting purposes. The mark-to-market committee has launched a project designed to facilitate this valuation, and LSTA has retained LPC to collect bid and offer price information from individual LSTA member-firms on a confidential basis, and to prepare aggregate average statistics for monthly dissemination to eligible LSTA members. The procedures that are followed are set forth in the 'Revised Statement of Procedures for Collection and Dissemination of Loan Valuation Information', published by the LSTA.
- *Lawyers working group* The lawyers working group was formed in mid-1996 in order to assist the other committees to identify, analyse and make recommendations with respect to the significant legal issues affecting existing and proposed market practices. The committee's first project focused on the disclosure of confidential information in connection with the trading of loan assets. To date, the committee has drafted proposed classifications and definitions of syndicate and borrower confidential information, as well as general policies regarding disclosure of such information in connection with trading activities. These definitions will be incorporated into the association's code of conduct during 1998. The committee has also devoted considerable effort to refining the binding oral trade agreement. It has also

provided invaluable assistance to the distressed debt, syndications and settlement committees in their efforts to establish efficient market practices within the boundaries of the law.

LMA

The establishment of the LSTA inspired the formation of the LMA in 1996 in London with the objective of fostering an environment in the Euromarkets that would facilitate the constructive development of a secondary market for loans.

The association was established to bring greater clarity, efficiency, and liquidity to the relatively under-developed secondary market that existed at the time and to enable more efficient loan portfolio management.

The use of Internet and web technology are central to the tying together of a hitherto disparate and fragmented community into a liquid market.

The LMA represents a group of bankers who are influencing the way the debt markets are conducting their business. What had traditionally been a people driven paper intensive business has migrated to the Internet for sake of communications, information diffusion, and loan syndications and trading. While actual transaction processing is not within their remit, their use of the Internet has resulted in increasing trading liquidity in the market and a forum and meeting place for bankers to coordinate discussions, transmission of information, and market developments.

The use of the Internet and the LMA web site, which has a public front and a members only front, is a key component of this strategy.

LMA objectives

Five initial aims were detailed at the outset:

- To standardize and simplify the sale of loan assets.
- To establish a market standard for settlement procedures.
- To establish codes of practice for market activity.

- To establish a loan valuation mechanism.
- To persuade borrowers, banks and other market participants of the merits of a more structured and liquid loan market.

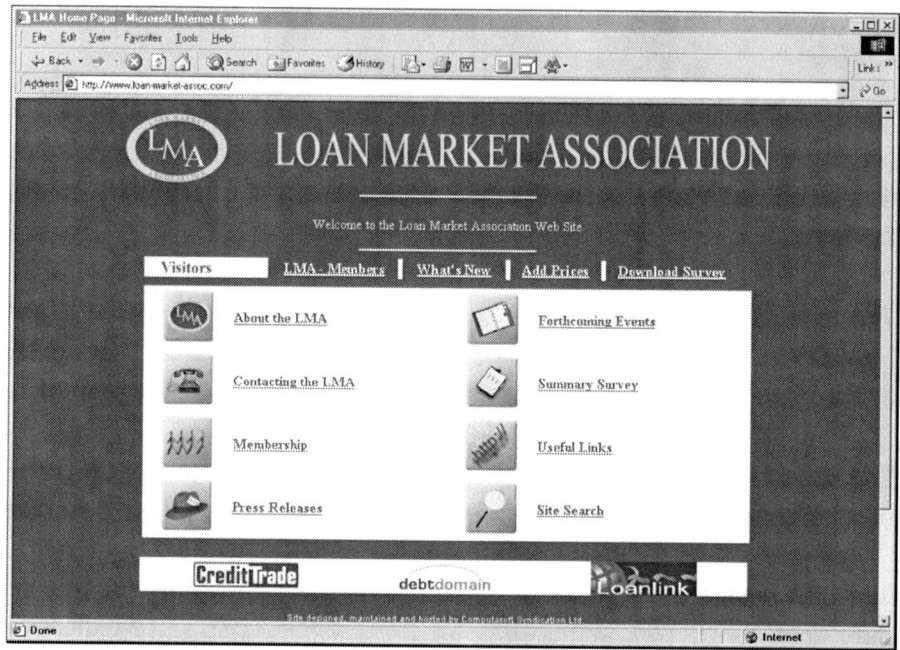

This initiative was clearly well timed as 1997 saw a rapid growth in the secondary loan activity in the Euromarkets, with volumes increasing to a level estimated at over USD 20 bn for the year, rising to USD 28 bn in 1999.

The LMA has expanded its activities to include all aspects of the primary and secondary syndicated loan markets. The LMA sees its mission as becoming the authoritative voice of the syndicated loan market in Europe vis-à-vis banks, borrowers, regulators, and other affected parties.

LMA committees

The LMA is organized around several committees, the main ones being:

- *Distressed debt committee* To help create an efficient market for distressed debt by the development of standard documentation for distressed debt trades.

Secondary loan markets

- *Documentation committee*   To create documentation for the primary and secondary loan markets.
- *Loan portfolio management committee*   To make proposals addressing loan trading issues so as to promote liquidity in the secondary credit markets.
- *Settlements*   To develop standard trading, settlement and operational procedures for the administration and trading of loan assets in the primary and secondary market.
- *Systems and technology*   To remain informed of technological innovations of relevance to the syndicated loan markets and to act as a contact point for service providers.

Main achievements

- Produced standard confirmations, terms and conditions and a variety of transfer documents for both bank debt and claims.
- Produced user guide for the above, including comparison between LMA and LSTA standards (Europe and USA).
- New documentation sent to members and posted on the web site.
- Events diary created on the web site to flag conferences and events.
- Established co-operation agreements with a number of e-trading platforms to foster use of LMA documents.
- Ongoing programme of upgrades to web site.
- Weekly pricing information posted on the LMA web site from April 1999.
- Agreements concluded with major financial publishers to show the summary survey in magazines and on electronic information services.
- Pricing graphs for individual loans available on web site valuation survey.
- Percentage price change index posted on web site.
- Feeds from Standard & Poor's (S&P) Ratings Services and Moody's Investors Service Ltd into valuation survey.
- Links to loanware information on deals on web site valuation survey.

Future aims

- Work with LSTA and APLMA towards harmonization of documentation and market practices.

- Promote recommended forms of primary documentation.
- Raise the profile of the LMA in continental Europe and the Middle East and within member organizations.
- Improve two-way communication with members.
- Develop a closer dialogue with LSTA and APLMA.
- Support entry of non-bank investors into the syndicated loan market.
- Loan portfolio management.
- Improve communication with similar groups in other major financial centres.
- To promote the use of leading edge technology to establish the concept of 'straight-through-processing' for trade settlement systems.
- To facilitate a fair and consistent trading environment and enhance liquidity within the secondary loan market.
- Develop total return and ratings indices.
- Develop a loan pricing calculator.

Syndicated loans and credit rating agencies

The introduction of credit ratings into the syndicated loan markets in the past 5 years is symptomatic of the changes in the syndicated loan market from a traditional, bespoke relationship-based 'bank loan market' to a more commoditized investor-driven 'loan market'. These developments warrant close examination, since they place as indispensable intermediaries in the syndicated loan markets entities (credit rating agencies) that have received much criticisms due to their inability accurately to forecast risk, their monopoly situation, predatory practices, and dysfunctions as noted by the US Senate Hearings on the Enron debacle and International Monetary Fund.

As is usually the case, this evolution first manifested itself in the US markets and is now striving to impose itself in the developed capital markets in Europe. The evolution of the US syndicated loan market from a private, relationship oriented credit market to a commoditized securities-style market has been proceeding steadily for several years. One noteworthy aspect has been the dramatic increase in the number of credit ratings assigned to syndicated loans. This is illustrated by the growth in rating syndicated loans – S&P notes for example that starting from a base of zero 6 years ago, it now rates the loans of about 1200 companies.

Although not yet as pervasive as in the public bond markets, S&P claims that its ratings are becoming 'increasingly expected on larger syndicated loans' although they cite no statistical evidence supporting this claim or identify who these ratings are increasingly expected by. While rating growth is strong across the board, S&P notes that it is particularly pronounced among larger loans, with 89% of loan facilities larger than USD 750 mn having been rated in 2001, up from only 57% just 3 years earlier.

The following table from S&P illustrates these trends.

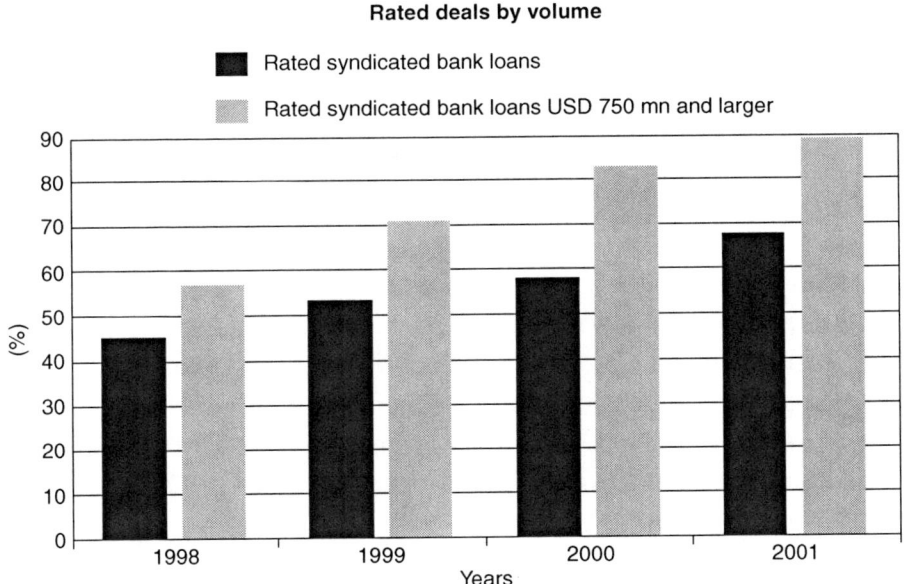

Source: S&P.

'Efficient' vs. 'inefficient' markets

The rise in loan ratings reflects the increased commoditization of the syndicated lending markets due to the implementation of standardized boilerplate loan syndication contracts fostered by the LMA and LSTA, akin to the standardized Master ISDA securities dealer agreements. These have been making considerable inroads in the US and European capital markets.

Outside the US and Europe (where a similar evolution is well under way), loan markets are still largely relationship based and thus 'inefficient' (according to S&P), by market standards. It is worth noting that these leading arguments do not account for facts, for example that 'inefficient' markets by definition would have fewer participants not because of the evolved (or unevolved) state of the markets but simply due to the lack of density of players in the market as a consequence of the lack of depth of the economy. In other words, developing countries markets are not 'inefficient' because they have not adopted credit ratings for syndicated loans but simply because the depth of the market and number of players in a shallow market does not warrant the introduction of credit ratings since the market for trading in commoditized loans simply does not exist.

S&P of course is not going to make this distinction in its literature since it is eager to tap into lucrative markets and position itself as an indispensable intermediary (thus imposing its monopoly situation into new sectors) irrespective of whether there is an perceived need for credit ratings either by issuers or participants. It is important to consider these elements which are glossed over if not entirely omitted in rating agency literature and consider their pronouncements not as gospel but merely marketing driven. Consider S&P distinction between 'efficient' and 'inefficient' markets for example:

- An efficient market must have widely available information about the issuers and the transactions, numerous participants, clear-cut roles for issuers, investors and intermediaries, and an established infrastructure to support primary and secondary distribution of securities.
- An inefficient market, by contrast, would likely have fewer participants, deals that are individually negotiated between principals that already have a relationship with each other and without reference to the

terms of comparable deals (since there is little information available about comparable deals), and the roles of the intermediary (i.e. a banker) and investor generally would be filled by the same institution.

S&P offers one value-loaded analysis of what characterizes an 'inefficient' market (i.e. the 'old' loan market) and 'efficient' one (the new loan market).

It is important to consider that rating syndicated loans offers S&P considerable scope to increase revenues by positioning themselves as indispensable intermediaries into new and hitherto untapped markets.

Since the US Senate Hearings[1] and numerous industry critics have lambasted the credit rating agencies for dysfunctional behaviour and inability properly to assess risks in areas in which they claim to have a 50+ year track record[2], one can receive S&P's arguments about the necessity of introducing credit ratings for syndicated loans with a healthy dose of scepticism, especially in view of the Senate Hearings' requirements for the SEC to address issues relating to credit rating agencies in the wake of the Sarbanes–Oxley Act[3].

---

[1] *'You know, Mom and Pop can read these public documents, and it seems that what we are learning from all of this is that there is really not much value-added for the average investor in looking at either what the analysts are saying or what the raters are doing; that when you have a complex set of documents, that you don't really go behind the documents, even though you have a right to'.* Sen. Fred Thompson Rating The Raters: Enron And The credit rating agencies US Senate Hearing Before The Committee On Governmental Affairs, 20 March 2002.
[2] *Several Directors noted that key international credit rating agencies had failed to foresee the Asian crisis and then aggravated it when they subsequently moved to sharply lower the credit ratings of countries.* International Monetary Fund 1999 Annual Report, Chapter 3, page 26.
[3] Section 702(b) of the Sarbanes–Oxley Act of 2002 requires the US Securities and Exchange Commission to prepare a report regarding the credit rating agencies as follows (extract of act). Section 702 Commission study and report regarding credit rating agencies.
(a) Study required:
(1) *In general* The Commission shall conduct a study of the role and function of credit rating agencies in the operation of the securities market.
(2) *Areas of consideration* The study required by this subsection shall examine:
　　(A) the role of credit rating agencies in the evaluation of issuers of securities;
　　(B) the importance of that role to investors and the functioning of the securities markets;
　　(C) any impediments to the accurate appraisal by credit rating agencies of the financial resources and risks of issuers of securities;
　　(D) any barriers to entry into the business of acting as a credit rating agency, and any measures needed to remove such barriers;
　　(E) any measures which may be required to improve the dissemination of information concerning such resources and risks when credit rating agencies announce credit ratings; and

For example, diversity is what characterized the syndicated loan markets. If S&P have their way, it will be akin to having all syndicated loans pass through a single credit rating clearinghouse, fostering a market characterized by a monolithic view as opposed to diversified and multilateral view enabling diversification of heterogeneous risk.

It is also placing lead manager banks in a position of not only needing to conform to a monolithic view of what characterizes acceptable risk, but also of relying on credit rating information of little added value[4] and dubious analytical accuracy[5]. Refer to the BBC article 'who knew what' by Orla Ryan on page 162 on this matter and contrast this with S&P claims as to the market demand for their ratings.

There is also the matter that credit rating agencies such as S&P have been considered as levers of the US government and foreign policy agenda[6]. It is indeed perhaps due to these developments that S&P notes the slower 'take-up' of syndicated loan ratings in the European markets.

(F) any conflicts of interest in the operation of credit rating agencies and measures to prevent such conflicts or ameliorate the consequences of such conflicts.
(b) Report required: The Commission shall submit a report in the study required by subsection (a) to the President, the Committee on Financial Services of the House of Representatives, and the Committee on Banking, Housing, and Urban Affairs of the Senate not later than 180 days after the date of enactment of this Act.

[4] The low value-added approach of opinions emitted by analysts with no set of qualifications is confirmed by the following quote from Moody's employee Fran Laserson: *Largely, the financial information on which we base our ratings is publicly filed information... We also have meetings with the issuers, who may choose to share issues with us, it is up to them, they will choose their level of disclosure* BBC News Online 1 February 2002, Who knew what?

[5] *When asked by Committee staff whether they considered as a qualitative factor in their analysis whether the company was engaging in aggressive accounting, the agencies indicated that they rely on the auditors' work. This was consistent with their testimony at the hearing. In the Committee staff interviews, the credit rating analysts resisted staff's suggestion that a company's accounting methods should be part of their analysis, because even when financial statements comply with Generally Accepted Accounting Principles (GAAP), they nevertheless may not present all the information an investor would want to know, or all the information a credit rater would want to know. This is troubling, because the fact that a company may be using the flexibility of GAAP to hide problems should be a consideration, particularly if the credit raters take a long-term view.* From 'Financial Oversight of Enron: The SEC and Private-Sector Watchdogs Report of the Staff to the Senate Committee on Governmental Affairs'; 8 October 2002; http://www.senate.gov/~gov_affairs/100702watchdogsreport.pdf

[6] *Iran dropped by US rating agency: International rating agency Moody's has withdrawn its sovereign credit ratings for Iran after pressure from the US Government. President George W Bush has claimed Iran is part of an 'axis of evil' and has continued to economic impose sanctions.* BBC News Article of 3 June 2002: http://news.bbc.co.uk/2/hi/business/2023568.stm

Acknowledging these issues however would lead to a host of thorny questions.

Consider the S&P table below, filled with loaded, albeit ambiguous, judgements. Having 20 banks each undertaking their own independent research in 'old' markets (old is bad) is labelled by S&P in negative terms as 'no credit ratings or third party research' while the new (new is good) markets have independent data and research (referring to S&P as 'independent'). This is at considerable odds with the previous footnotes from the IMF and Senate Hearings on Enron and the failure of credit rating agencies to anticipate risks.

Being an industry development however, it is important to understand the pros and cons surrounding this new market development. One major impact is that the bank's ability to underwrite and market syndicated loans will now be subordinated to the market power and agendas of the US rating agencies. Banks paradoxically, are weakening their autonomy and market position as underwriters by acquiescing in the credit rating agencies' positioning themselves as self appointed indispensable intermediaries in the syndicated loan markets.

Loan market characteristics Then and Now

'Old' loan market	'New' loan market
Opaque (information closely held)	Transparent (information widely available)
No credit ratings or third party research	Credit ratings, independent data and research
Club lending with specialized credit knowledge	Numerous investors
Negotiated or 'relationship' pricing	Competitive pricing with comparative pricing information available
Bank plays both intermediary and investor roles	Intermediary and investor roles more distinct
'Buy-and-hold' lenders	Portfolio theory and secondary trading used to manage portfolios
Documentation and distribution protocols unique to agent bank	Standardized instruments and established trading protocols

For a more thorough look at the world of credit rating agencies, one can consult *The Ratings Game* and *Understanding International Bank Risk*, both books by Andrew Fight and published by Wiley and Sons.

Who knew what?
by BBC News Online's Orla Ryan

A suspicious mood has settled on Wall Street in the wake of the Enron bankruptcy.

The collapse of the company feted by investment bankers and politicians has led many to question why no one saw it coming. As the US Congress debates the role of those who kept the energy giant company, attention is also turning to the credit rating agencies. The Enron collapse has highlighted the role of these agencies, who provide guidance to investors on a borrower's creditworthiness.

'Lots of people were there at the time beyond auditors. There were rating agencies reporting up to a very short time before the collapse of Enron', Andersen UK's managing partner John Ormerod told the BBC's World Business Report.

While Andersen's excuses may seem lame, as the auditor tries to deflect attention from its own role, other critics are making similar noises.

Blame game

The analysis provided by rating agencies is influential in determining the interest rates that borrowers pay on their debt. Rating agencies such as Moody's, S&P and Fitch grade borrowers – both companies and countries – as to their creditworthiness.

Who knew what

Moody dismisses suggestions they were in a better position to know than other analysts. 'Largely, the financial information on which we base our ratings is publicly filed information', Moody's Fran Laserson said. 'We also have meetings with the issuers, who may choose to share issues with us, it is up to them, they will choose their level of disclosure', she added.

The three big agencies have already indicated that they are looking at tweaking the way they do business. Even as the job descriptions are being tweaked, Fitch's Bob Grossman is clear that agencies provide 'leadership'.

But in rumour-driven markets, prices rise and fall, and it can seem that rating agencies take their lead from traders, rather than the other way around.

'If they are only reacting to changes of risk that markets have already priced in, they become less useful', Bank of America's Juliet Sampson said.

The agencies – more highly visible than other analysts and hence more vulnerable to criticism – cannot be seen to be reacting to market whim.

Deja vu

The tricky point for the agencies is that we have been here before. The rating agencies also faced criticism for acting too slowly at the time of the Asian and Russian crises.

Bank of America's Ms Sampson believes that country rating changes have less impact than before, partly due to 'a loss of credibility in the last round of crises' in Russia and Asia. For some investors, the agency's word is a rubber stamp and nothing else.

'Most city analysts don't think much of rating agencies is the truth of the matter they use rating agencies as an insurance device', one seasoned market watcher said.

'If things go sour, the pension fund administrator can say we checked with the rating agency and they gave it a clean bill of health, in other words it is not our fault'.

Other market drivers

We consider three elements impacting this development: Market-flex pricing, the new Basel Capital Accords, and Secondary Asset Trading.

- Market-flex pricing is a new development in the syndicated loan markets which allows the syndicator to vary the interest rate margin (i.e. the spread over the base rate, which is generally London InterBank Offered Rate) by a certain amount, often 25 basis points (bps) or 50 bps, as dictated by 'market conditions' at the time of closing the loan. This in a way defeats the agent banks' arguments that they should be selected for a loan syndication based on their deep understanding of the market and its price levels and characteristics for various categories of risk. S&P claims that syndicating banks have embraced credit ratings as a way to broaden the potential investor base (summarize complex risks in a simple to understand alphabetic classification scheme) and therefore improve the pricing they can offer to issuers.
- The New Basel Capital Accords, once completed and put into effect, are expected to accelerate the banking industry's movement toward risk-based and market-driven methods of bank management and supervision. Virtually all of these various methodologies have one thing in common: a need for consistent, objective, and comparable means of measuring credit risk across asset classes, institutions, and geographic and political frontiers.
- Secondary trading, besides being an attractive business in its own right to the large dealers, has facilitated the growth of the market in many ways. Banks can more confidently adopt sophisticated loan portfolio management techniques if they know there is an actual secondary market they can use to balance and re-balance their portfolios as needed. Many of the non-bank institutional loan buyers, being traditional portfolio managers rather than banks with large credit departments, are comfortable knowing that they can sell out of credits at the hint of trouble or a credit downgrade.

Impact of credit ratings on syndicated loans markets

S&P has identified winners and losers in these new developments.

- One clear winner has been the issuer, the corporate borrower who now can tap hundreds of potential investors instead of the handful of banks that previously may have been part of its lending 'club'. Other things being equal, one can usually negotiate a more attractive deal when there are dozens of potential providers than if there are just a few. But to achieve this advantage, a borrower has had to sacrifice some privacy, and allow itself to be known – via the credit rating process and the research provided to its loan investors – to that wider investor audience.
- The other big winner has been the large syndicating bank which has made the transition from being a 'buy-and-hold' lender (using its balance sheet to earn spread income), to being a true investment bank that earns fee income by underwriting deal after deal and offloading the loans onto the market.
- Non-bank investors who previously now have access to loan assets that were hitherto unavailable, and can now access loans in geographic areas and industries that they may not have previously been comfortable with.
- Disadvantaged entities include traditional banks that were the typical 'buy-and-hold' relationship lenders who have not made the transition to the role of underwriter/syndicator. These banks have seen their spread lending revenue shrink, because they are now competing with dozens of new institutional investors for each new loan. Particularly negatively affected have been banks lending to specialized sectors (e.g. project finance) that required a great deal of specialized knowledge from highly skilled lenders.
- Corporate issuers who value control and want to have close, direct relationships with their lenders may be uncomfortable with broadly distributed syndicated loans, held by anonymous institutional investors, and with whom a chief financial officer has little or no contact. While the better terms and cheaper pricing may make up for this in most cases, some companies may prefer the greater control, especially those that anticipate covenant breaches or an ongoing need to renegotiate loan terms.

S&P believes that the trends described here are likely to intensify in North America and Europe, where they are well advanced, and to spread throughout the world but again, do not provide any statistical or economic arguments to suggest that countries with their own economic systems necessarily wish to espouse economic models developed elsewhere.

Recent developments in the European syndicated loan market

The European market is now showing clear signs of building the core characteristics of a more investor-driven loan market. However, many of these features are recent arrivals and require time and market application to 'season' before other essential features of such a market – in particular comparable pricing data and secondary trading liquidity – develop and provide necessary support.

The principal features characterizing the development of the European syndicated loan market can be summarized as follows:

- *The growth in the non-bank investor base* The European market is seeing strong growth in participation by non-bank investors. Insurance companies, pension funds and arbitrage vehicles are now seeking out attractive risk-adjusted returns available from senior secured loan participations in leveraged buy-out transactions.
- *The growth in ratings* While the penetration of bank loans in the European loan market remains low when compared to the US, the incidence of specific loan ratings on new financings has increased significantly over the past 18 months. For calendar year 2001, S&P assigned ratings on over USD 45 bn, or 10% of new syndicated financing in Europe, and, at the end of calendar year 2001, the total volume of loans outstanding in the market with a S&P ratings was in excess of USD 165 bn.
- *Club lending and 'relationship' pricing practices* These 'old market' practices are slowly declining in importance, but remain a significant feature of the European market. This is due to traditional 'old Europe' factors such an over-banked market (employment legislation and protection); multiple sovereign states; and, to date, a lack of cross-border banking consolidation due to cultural distinction. US-oriented S&P believes that Europe will increasingly adopt a more commoditized

and relationship-free market-based approach to pricing, but this may only be wishful thinking as opposed to an analysis of political realities and differing legal systems.
- *Comparable pricing data and secondary trading liquidity*   Historically, the tradition of 'take-and-hold' lending by European commercial banks and the presence of restrictive assignment and transfer language, meant that there was little interest in secondary loan trading.

The London-based LMA has been in the forefront in its efforts to standardize and simplify loan and transfer documentation. It is important to realize however that while London may be the largest financial centre in Europe, it does not coordinate banking practice on a pan European basis and the take-up of a unified pan European secondary loan market may still be a way off, and may end up quite different from the US model.

Glossary

Acceleration The action taken by an agent, on the instructions of the participants, to call for early repayment of a syndicated loan following an event of default by the borrower.

Accounting period Period of time from one balance sheet to the next. Period of the income statement, usually 1 year.

Accounts receivable financing Procedure whereby a specialized financial institution or bank makes loans against the pledge of accounts receivable.

Accrued interest The interest earned since the latest interest payment due but not yet paid.

Accrued interest payable Interest owing on loans or other financial assets and thereby passed through the income statement but which has not yet been remitted by the bank.

Accrued interest receivable Interest accrued on loans or other financial assets and thereby passed through the income statement but which has not been received by the bank.

Acquisition The purchase of assets or a controlling interest in a company by another company. It is generally used to describe cash transactions as opposed to equity transactions.

ADB Asian Development Bank, headquartered in Manila, Philippines.

Administrative agent The US term for the arranger of a syndicated transaction.

Advance A generic term for the ways in which a bank lends money, whether loan, overdraft, or discount.

Advance payment guarantee A guarantee issued by a bank on behalf of, say, a contractor to protect the buyer and which provides for repayment of the advance payments in the event of the contractor's failure to carry out the contract terms.

Glossary

Agent The bank which acts as agent of all the participants and manages the facility once it has been signed. The agent may also be the arranger of the loan and a participant in the loan.

AIBD Association of International Bond Dealers.

Alternate borrowers A syndicated loan facility may contain an ability, for more than one borrower to draw the loan. Alternate borrowers are usually subsidiaries or associates of the principal borrower...

Amortization (1) The expending of an intangible asset in a company's income statement over a period of time judged to be the economic life of the asset. Like depreciation, amortization is a non-cash expense.

Amortization (2) The paying off of a loan in staged payments (repayment instalments).

Arrangement fees For their efforts in arranging a deal, banks collect arrangement fees. These fees are attractive for the bank because they represent revenues that do not have to be generated by the balance sheet, which are subject to capital adequacy (Cooke) ratios.

Arranger The bank which arranges a syndicated loan, negotiates the terms and conditions with the borrower, and syndicates the loan amongst the participants. The arranger may also act as agent bank but need not. It may also be a participant in the loan.

Arranging banks The banks which arrange the financing on behalf of a corporate borrower. Usually, the banks commit to underwrite the whole amount only if they are unable to place the deal fully. Typically, however, they place the bulk of the facility and retain a portion on their books for themselves.

Asset liability management (ALM) A technique to match cash flows, sand maturities of assets and liabilities to maximize return and minimize the interest rate risk from mismatching.

Asset quality Asset quality refers to the ability of a bank's assets, especially its loans, to continue to perform according to their terms and generate net interest income for the bank. An evaluation of a bank's asset quality includes not only quantitative measures of the bank's problem loans but also qualitative elements such as the bank's policy for allocating loan loss provisions, lending strategies, credit review policies and procedures, loan portfolio composition, and general credit culture.

Asset trading In banking, this refers to buying and selling loans on the secondary markets. Although loans are generally viewed as illiquid assets, banks may be able to trade loans (usually blue chip although trading in distressed debt also exists). Typically this depended on having no prohibition in the loan agreement but typically, clauses permitting asset trading are now included as standard clauses in the loan agreements due to the initiatives of industry groups such as the Loan Marketing Association in London. The reason for trading in this market may be that a bank desires to reconfigure its loan portfolio. Asset trading is the logical continuation of syndicated lending.

Asset-backed loans A loan which is supported by assets owned by the issuer of the debt and usually placed with a trustee.

Assignment An agreement to transfer all of the rights (but not the obligations) under the contract to a new lender via an assignment agreement. In the USA the term can also denote the transfer of obligations.

Audit A process of examination of financial statements and the underlying accounting. An independent audit will provide a systematic investigation of the accounting systems and controls to ensure compliance with prescribed accounting and auditing standards.

Availability period Time period after the signing of the loan agreement during which the borrower, having satisfied conditions precedent, is permitted to drawdown advances.

Back-to-back loan Companies with surplus liquidity in one currency may wish to obtain funds in another, for investment or expansion, by employing their own surplus resources without conversion or incurring exchange exposure, or without incurring increased interest costs by borrowing unmatched funds; this may be arranged by means of a parallel, or back to back loan.

Bad loan A loan which is not expected to be collectable in full. This term is often used to describe non-performing loans, or impared loans.

Balance sheet A statement reflecting the financial position at a specific moment in time.

Balloon payment Large final payment (e.g. when a loan is repaid in instalments).

Bank A financial institution licensed to accept money deposits and make loans (often called a 'commercial bank' to differentiate it from a securities house or investment bank).

Bank for International Settlements The Bank for International Settlements (BIS) was established in 1930 and is known as the 'Central Banks'

Central Bank'. It accepts deposits and makes loans to its member banks, and acts as a source of information for issues related to international capital movements. The BIS is based in Basle, Switzerland, and has provided a forum for the Basle Committee on Banking Supervision, a group of regulators from the Group of 10 (G10) countries which has been involved in promoting uniform rules on bank capital adequacy, risk management, and bank supervision.

Bank run A bank run is a panic in which depositors, fearing that a bank is experiencing financial difficulty, queue up at a bank's offices demanding the return of their deposits (usually by then far too late). This vulnerability to panic underscores the importance of public confidence in the banking system.

Banking crisis A loss of confidence which threatens the breakdown or collapse of a banking system's ability to function as a supplier of credit and payment system. A banking crisis typically features capital flight (withdrawal of assets and transfer of these assets abroad or conversion into foreign currency) and a liquidity crunch (insufficient funds to enable banks to act as a provider of capital). Such a crisis can result in corporate failures and a fall in overall economic activity.

Banking environment The business and regulatory and competitive environment in which a bank operates. The banking environment includes elements such as country and sovereign risk, macro-economic factors, political factors, competition, consolidation, interest rate environment, entry of new players, changes in banking regulation and legislation, changes in capitalization requirements, etc. all basically macro-economic elements exterior to the bank.

Basis (or reference) rate The benchmark cost of funds to which the margin will be added or deducted to determine the total rate payable by the borrower (e.g. (London InterBank Offer Rate) LIBOR, London InterBank Bid Rate (LIBID), and Prime are basis rates).

Basis point One 100th of one cent.

Basle Accord The Basle Capital Accord of 1988, formally known as 'International Convergence of Capital Measurement and Capital Standards'. The Basle Accord attempts to apply uniform measures in a heterogeneous international environment. The Basle Accord is in the process of being revised under the 'Basle 2' arrangements – in which a first consultative document was issued in 1999, and a final consultative document in 2001, with approval in 2001 and final implementation in 2004.

Basle Agreement The 1988 agreement, made under the auspices of the BIS, under which different types of banking assets are weighted and applied against the capital of banks.

Basle Committee The Basle Committee on Banking Supervision comprises a panel of regulators from the Group of 10 (G10) countries that convenes at the BIS in Basle, Switzerland. It should be noted that these two organizations are separate organizations. The committee established the first standards for international capital adequacy of banks.

BIS The Bank for International Settlements, the main global banking regulator.

Boilerplate Clauses found regularly in loan documentation which are standard and vary little from agreement to agreement.

Borrower risk Risks pertaining to the company, including management, profitably, non-performance, and bankruptcy: all factors relating to the borrower.

Break-even analysis Analysis of the level of sales at which a project would just break even (e.g. project revenues cover project costs).

Bullet loans A loan whose interest is payable at intervals agreed in the loan agreement, and whose principal is repayable in a lump sum (bullet repayment) at final maturity. There are no principal repayments along the way. The source of repayment is usually a new facility which is put into place.

Call deposits Deposits which are repayable on the demand either of the bank or of the depositor.

Cap An option strategy that sets a ceiling on the holder's interest rate exposure.

Capital and reserves (shareholders' funds/net worth) The value the owners have invested in the business. This is represented by share capital and reserves.

Capital markets The market for debt and equity instruments.

Capitalization Long-term debt, preferred stock, plus net worth.

Capitalized interest Accrued interest (and margin) which is not paid but added ('rolled up') at the end of each interest period to the principal amount lent (e.g. in relation to balloon repayment).

Cash flow lending Lending whose repayment is to come from the borrower's future cashflow.
Collateral See Security.
Commitment fee The fee payable to participants on the undrawn portion of a syndicated loan facility.
Commitment period The period, defined in the loan agreement, by which time the syndicated loan must be drawn. If the loan is not fully drawn in this period, the undrawn commitments of the participants are automatically cancelled.
Common stock Ordinary shares.
Company (corporation) A legal entity with perpetual succession.
Contingent liabilities Items which do not represent a liability on the balance sheet at the time of statement date but which could do so in the future. Such items include guarantees issued in favour of third parties, and lawsuits currently in progress whose outcome is uncertain.
Cooke ratio The capital adequacy or risk weighted asset ratios prescribed by the Basle Committee on Banking Supervision.
Corporate lending Lending to large and multinational corporations. Smaller and medium sized companies are referred to as 'SME' lending.
Cost of funds A term sometimes used as the basis for a loan pricing, particularly when the source of funding is uncertain or includes reserve asset costs. A precise definition of what is meant by this term should be established if it is to be of any practical value; it should be noted that the normal funding cost of a commercial loan is the offered rate, being the rate which the bank has to pay to another bank in the market for the funds obtained for the purpose.
Country exposure Country exposure is the amount of an institution's total investment and/or claims on borrowers in a specific country, direct as well as indirect.
Country limit Country limits are the numerical amounts up to which an institution such as a bank or company is willing to take an exposure to in a particular country.
Country rating Country ratings are the result of the individual appraisal of a particular country in view of its standing to honour its foreign debts in relation to other countries or groups of countries.
Covenant An agreement by a borrower to perform certain acts (such as the provision of financial statements or the respecting of a financial

ratio) or to refrain from certain acts (such as incurring further indebtedness beyond an agreed level).

Credit   The process of taking a risk for the settlement of an obligation in the future.

Credit approval process   The loan approval procedure within a lending institution.

Credit limit/credit lines   The limits up to which a bank is prepared to lend money or grant credit to a customer. Credit limits/credit lines are usually used for internal management purposes and guidelines are not normally a legal commitment, only a willingness to do business.

Credit risk   The risk of losses arising from defaults by the counter party.

Credit scoring   Technique used to evaluate a potential borrower according to a pre-defined matrix procedure (e.g. matrix such as the Altman Bankruptcy Predictor using Multiple Discriminant Analysis to generate a Z-Score). Usually used in retail banking and credit card processing, also used in evaluating corporates.

Creditor   Payable, account payable, liability. Money owed to other parties. Current or long-term liability.

Debt equity ratio   The ratio of a company's ordinary share capital to its fixed interest capital, including debentures, loan stock, and preference shares; calculations are often simply based on the ratio of ordinary shares plus retained reserves to prior charge capital.

Debt ratings   The classification of a company's financial (credit) standing by specialist agencies such as Moody's and Standard & Poor's (e.g. A+, A, A−, B+, B, B−, C).

Debt securities   An instrument denoting an obligation by the issuer to pay the current and/or future holder(s) the due interest and principal.

Debt service   The payment of interest, fees, and principal in accordance with the loan agreement.

Default   The debtor notifies the creditor that he will definitely cease making any further service payments because he cannot, or does not, want to pay.

Default interest clause   A clause providing for interest to continue to accrue on an overdue debt, usually at an enhanced rate. The clause may be void as a penalty under English law if the rate of interest imposed does not represent a genuine estimate of the loss being suffered by the lender.

Glossary

Default, event of Failure to fulfil the conditions of a contract (see Event of default and cross default).

Deposits Current liabilities of the bank in the form of current account funds or monies at call, notice, or fixed term.

Disclaimer Statement made by the arranger and contained in documents such as Information Memoranda which asserts that certain information provided in the prospectus was supplied by the borrower, and is therefore not the responsibility of the arranger.

Documentation risk The risk of non-repayment due to defect in the loan agreement or security arrangements. This can arise due to faulty drafting, mitigating circumstances, juridically non-enforceable and faulty collateral, or guarantees which have expired and not been renewed. Analysts are not expected to assess legal issues, but are expected to obtain legal opinions when necessary and note them accordingly.

Drawdown The actual borrowing of money (advance) under the terms of a facility.

EBRD European Bank for Reconstruction and Development. The EBRD's London head office is noteworthy for its lavish premises and lobby: its new marble surfacing has been recently replaced with exquisite Italian marble. As a minor sideline, the EBRD is involved in financing the economic development of Eastern Europe.

Efficient market Market in which security prices reflect information instantaneously.

Equity An ownership interest in a company. Usually this is in the form of ordinary shares (European English) or common stock (American). Equities and bonds are the main basic types of 'securities'.

Event of default An event listed in the loan documentation which enables the lender to cancel the credit facility and declare all amounts owing by the debtor in the subject credit facility to be immediately due and payable. Events of default typically include non-payment of amounts due to the lender, breach of covenant, cross-default, insolvency, and material adverse change.

Evergreen facility A facility which is renewable from year to year.

Exchange rate The price of one currency in terms of another.

Exposure The extent to which a bank or institution is reliant on one or more counterparties as a result of trading transactions.

Facility The grant of availability of money at some future date in return for a fee.

Facility agent The agent of the banks in the syndicate who provides the committed facility, who fixes LIBOR, LIBID, and other reference rates and co-ordinates the banks.

Facility fee An annual percentage fee payable on a pro rata basis to banks providing a credit facility on the full amount of the facility, whether or not it is used.

Fee letter A very important document – sets out the fees to be paid to the arranging bank and/or agent. This is very confidential as often, not all fees paid are shared with the syndicate members.

Final maturity date The date for payment of the last repayment instalment.

Fixed rate loan A term loan for which the interest rate for the whole period is determined at the outset.

Floor An option strategy that sets a floor on the holder's exposure to the underlying stock.

FOREX Foreign exchange market from spot or forward 'exchange dealings'.

Front end costs Commission, fees, or other payments that are taken at the 'outset' of a loan, such as, for example, discounting; the front end charges for capital issues are very considerable and in calculating the total cost, a borrower should be aware of the additional cost of being short of such disbursements at the outset when compared with the cost of interest payments that are payable after the loan period and not before.

Governing law The legal system to which the terms and conditions of a transaction are subject.

Grace period A period of days within which the borrower is allowed to remedy a breach or failure of payment before that breach or failure becomes an event of default; confusingly, can also mean the period before the first repayment instalment is due (e.g. repayment by five semi-annual instalments, 2 years' grace, which means that the loan is repaid at 6-monthly intervals starting after 2 years).

Grossing up The provision in the facility agreements whereby the borrower agrees that in the event of an imposition of any withholding or similar taxes in its country of incorporation, it will pay such additional amount as will ensure that the banks are effectively free of such taxes.

Guarantee An undertaking in writing by one person (the guarantor) given to another, usually a bank (the creditor) to be answerable for the debt of a third person (the debtor) to the creditor, upon default of the debtor. Different from but usually coupled with, an indemnity.

Information memorandum A memorandum produced by the agent in consultation with the borrower and circulated to potential participants in a syndicated loan facility. It gives information on the borrower and its business sector and the structure of the proposed loan, and is designed to make the credit process of potential participants as easy and well informed as possible.

Intangible assets Assets which are not tangible and do not have an easily ascertainable value, e.g. goodwill, patents, and trademarks.

Interest The cost of money; money paid for the use of money.

Interest period The period by reference to which interest is paid, typically 1, 3, or 6 months as this tracks the interbank funding market. Interest is paid at a fixed rate during each period but is refixed at the start of the next period thus reflecting the change in market conditions.

Interest rate risk The change in capital values of the investment introduces a serious risk into what may be a safe investment. Due to increased capital risk, long-term investments provide higher returns than short term indicated by a positive yield term. Where long-term rates do not offer enhanced yields over short-term rates, a flat or inverted yield curve is seen.

Investment bank A financial institution which (normally) underwrites and trades securities and offers related advisory services. It may be part of, or affiliated with, a 'bank' (as defined above) – but not necessarily.

Lead manager A lead bank which syndicates or subparticipates a loan to various 'takers' (subparticipants) in the market.

LIBID The London InterBank Bid Rate: the rate at which banks buy deposits in the market.

LIBOR London InterBank Offer Rate. The interest rate at which major international banks in London lend to each other. (LIBID: London InterBank Bid Rate; LIMEAN: London InterBank Mean Rate.)

Limit Maximum exposure allowed in a currency, or to a counterparty, as set down internally by management.

Liquidity The ability to service debt and redeem or reschedule liabilities when they mature, and the ability to exchange other assets for cash.

Liquidity ratios The acid test and current ratios used to measure changes in liquidity between various accounting periods.

Liquidity risk The risk of losses arising from a derivative market becoming a liquid or where the difficulty or cost issues arise when closing the position.

Loan agreement The document which sets out the terms and conditions of the syndicated loan facility. It is signed by the borrower, the agent, and each of the participants. It is normally drafted by solicitors and is designed to cover every eventuality and describe every course of action which may arise during the life of the syndicated loan.

Majority banks A group of participants, whose votes usually consist of at least 66⅔% of the amount of the syndicated loan facility, who instruct the agent to take action (or not do so) on matters defined in the loan agreement.

Management accounting Part of the accounting system used to provide information for managing the business in a form required for internal use compared to financial accounting which is for external use and must reflect prescribed formats and content.

Management buy-out (MBO) The purchase of a business by its managers, usually part-financed by a syndicate of banks; may be several layers of debt, including mezzanine finance.

Margin The rate taken by the lender over the cost of funds, which effectively represents his profit and remuneration for taking the risk of the loan; also known as 'spread'.

Marketability The degree of investment demand for a particular asset offered at a given price.

MOF Multiple option facility – usually consisting of two or more options for the borrower to take loans (committed or through a tender panel procedure), swing line advances, bills of exchange, or notes.

Moratorium A moratorium is the unilateral declaration of the borrower that he is unable and/or unwilling to honour all or part of his obligations and thereby stops the servicing of his debts.

Multi-currency loan A loan where the borrower has the option to drawdown funds in more than one currency.

Negative pledge A covenant in a facility agreement by the borrower not to grant security over its assets to other creditors (since this would put those other creditors in a preferential position).

Net worth (owners' equity) The value owed by a business to its owners reflecting the difference between the total value of all assets and total of all liabilities. It is the value attributable to the owners in respect of the net financial position of the business.

Novation The transfer of rights and obligations from one entity to another, for example, following the substitution of a new debtor for an old debtor or of one bank for another under a loan facility by way of substitution (transfer) certificate.

Novation agreement A document which formally concludes the sale and transfer (by novation) of all 'rights and obligations' from an existing lender to a new lender.

Pari passu Literally 'at the same rate' – usually with reference to a borrower's or guarantor's obligations ranking equally with each other in an insolvency.

Participant A member of a syndicate of banks providing a syndicated loan.

Participation fee The fee payable to participants on the total amount of their commitments in a syndicated loan facility.

Pledge A delivery of chattels or a chose in action by a debtor to a creditor as security for his debt, the legal ownership remaining with the pledgor.

Political risk The exposure to a loss in cross-border lending, caused by political factors in a certain country, political factors which are, at least to some extent under the control of the government but not under the control of a private enterprise or individual.

Portfolio A bank's or investor's loan and investment assets.

Project finance The financing of a specific project on terms such that the banks will receive repayment out of cash flows generated by the project as opposed to the assets of the project sponsoring company.

Rating A letter grade signifying a debt's investment quality. Two widely known rating agencies are Moody's Investors Service and Standard & Poor's.

Ratio analysis Calculation of financial ratios as an aid to interpretation.

Reference banks   A group of banks (usually three) selected by the agent to quote their LIBOR (or other basis rate) on each rollover the average of which is taken as the rate applicable to the transaction.

Rescheduling   Rescheduling is a process by which the lender and the borrower agree to arrange new conditions for an existing loan agreement.

Return on assets (ROA)   A measure of a syndicated loan's profitability to the lenders. Return on assets (ROA) includes the margin, fees, and interest generated over the life of the facility. Since fees are allocated based on participation status, ROA varies from bank to bank.

Revolver/evergreen facility   A bank line of credit on which the customer (normally) pays a commitment fee and can drawdown and repay funds according to his needs. Normally, the line involves a firm commitment from the bank for a period of several years.

Risk asset weighting   The weighting of individual assets on or off the balance sheets of commercial banks for purposes of calculating compliance with capitalization adequacy ratios.

Rollover   The time when the interest rate of a floating rate loan is periodically reviewed at an agreed spread over, at, or under the currently prevailing LIBOR. In 'true/classic' revolving facilities, the loans are repaid and redrawn on each rollover so that each loan is a separate and discrete borrowing.

Secondary Market   The market which enables banks to trade in participations in syndicated loans after they have been finalized. This market enables banks to manage their portfolio levels and sector requirements in a convenient and simple way.

Secondary market   A market in which securities, bonds, or debt is traded after issue, with profits accruing to the trader rather than to the original issuer.

Secured debt   Debt backed by specified assets or revenues of the borrower. Banks can call on these assets if the borrower is unable to repay the loan.

Senior debt   Debt which has priority of repayment in a liquidation.

Special purpose vehicle (SPV)   A legal entity created for the completion of a specific project such as hotel, airport, or fund. Special purpose vehicles (SPVs) are used to isolate the entity legally and financially from other participants such as the shareholders.

… *Glossary*

Special purpose vehicle   A company formed especially for the purposes of a syndicated loan facility, which will draw the loan and subsequently receive income or assets to repay it. The assets and liabilities of the SPV are legally separated from other assets and liabilities of the borrowing group so that they may not be claimed by other creditors.

Statement of cash flow   A statement which reconciles movements in cash between two accounting periods.

Subordinated loan   A loan whose seniority in a liquidation scenario is lower than classic bank debt but higher than equity. Subordinated loans will usually be made for long periods and will usually not be callable. Bankers therefore consider subordinated loans as quasi equity since their ranking order of priority is superior.

Subparticipation   The sale of an asset where the subparticipant agrees to fund the loan and assume the credit risk but does not obtain any rights and obligations against the borrower. Subparticipations can either be public (acknowledged) or silent (unacknowledged).

Syndicate   A group of banks participating in a single credit facility. The level of commitment (underwriting or final take) and related title offered to banks invited into a syndicated transaction are defined by the following titles:

- arranger – a mandated bank responsible for originating, executing and in some cases underwriting a transaction;
- joint arrangers – a group of mandated banks, sharing roles and underwriting commitments, if any;
- lead manager – a bank committing to the highest level of participation;
- co-arranger – a second level mandated or underwriting bank;
- lead manager – a bank committing to the highest level of participation;
- manager – a bank committing to the second level of participation;
- co-manager – a bank committing to a third level of participation; and
- participant – a bank committing to the most junior level of participation.

Not all of these titles are available on all transactions.

Syndicate list The list of banks to be approached in the general syndication, following agreement between the arranger, the underwriter, if any, and the borrower.

Syndicated loan A loan made available by a group of banks in predefined proportions under the same credit facility.

Syndication The process of putting together the group of banks who will participate in the facility.

Term loan A loan with a fixed drawdown period and a repayment schedule, where the principal is normally repaid in equal instalments (usually 6 monthly).

Tombstone An advertisement which lists the managers and underwriters and sometimes the providers of a recently completed facility or issue.

Transfer risk Is the impossibility of transferring payments abroad (in foreign currency) because the government imposed exchange restrictions.

Ultra vires Literally 'beyond the powers' – relating to the capacity of a company to enter into a transaction as authorized by its articles of association. Ultra vires transactions are void from the outset.

Utilization fee The fee payable to participants on each drawdown of a syndicated loan.

Working capital The difference between current assets and current liabilities.

Index

accounting period 168
accrued interest 99, 168
agent 1, 19, 37, 115, 169
amortizing loans 69, 98, 99
arranger and the agent
   Condition Precedent 38
   documentation
      ancillary 38
      loan 38
   sharing information 37
   other appointments
      independent technical advisers 39
      security trustees 39
arranger 1, 19, 31, 37, 45–48, 169
Asian syndicated lending market
   Japanese leviathans 48

balloon repayment 69, 70, 98, 99
banks
   performance 43
Barclays Capital
   activities
      bonds market 63
bond market 9

borrower 2, 17, 54–57, 126
   alternate borrowers 7
covenant
   negative pledge 29
credit rating agencies
   Moody's 9
   Standard & Poor's (S&P) 9, 160
cross border transactions
   domestic funding constraints 7
event of default 29
experience 32
geographic location 32
information memorandum 29
margins and fees 10, 32
   financial information 10
   information memorandum 10
market presence
   financial magazines 12
participants
   bilateral relationships 11
placing power 31
restriction of negotiation
   accounting functions 8
sector 32
Special Purpose Vehicle

Index

borrower (cont.)
  see also SPV
    loan agreement 7
    ring-fenced 8
  speed of action
    short-time scale 32
  speed of finalization
    credit approval requirements 9
  structuring ability
    capital market instruments 31
    'one stop' service 31
  terms and conditions 9
  underwriting
    balance sheet capacity 33
British Telecommunications Company
  ability 87
  'next generation' 3G licence 87
  Vodafone AirTouch 85
bullet repayment 69, 70, 99

Condition Precedent 38
covenant violation
  costs 142
  renegotiation process 143
covenants
  acounting policies 139–140
  corporate treasurer 132
  disclosure of information 144–145
  economic rationale 133–134
  functioning 137–140
    monitoring compliance 137
    restriction of management 138
  management policy
    Burlington Northern Railroad Company's (BNR) 138
  objectives 131–132
  other issues 143–144

  private debt agreements 140
  restrictions
    longer-term loans 135
    standardized documentation 132
    tailoring accounting 135
      Financial Reporting Standards (FRS) 136
      Generally Accepted Accounting Principles (GAAP) 136
currency 69

dividend decisions 126

European syndicated loan market
  investor-driven loan market 166
  principle features 166–167
events of default
  clauses 130
  financial defaults 30
  material adverse change 131
  technical default 30
evergreen facilities
  evergreen notice period 72
  working capital 72

fee income
  commitment fee 15, 16, 103, 173
  participation fee 15, 16, 179
  off-fee payable 15
  utilization fee 15, 16, 182
fianancial decisions 126
financial covenants 130, 144
  accounting standards 145
financial statement disclosure
  objective
    users' information needs 144
  Securities and Exchange Commission (SEC) 145
foreign exchange 11

Index

industry sectors
  big 4 59
  domestic consumer driven 59
  financial sector 59
investment decisions 126

Japanese banks
  asset quality problems 49
  capitalization ratio 49

League tables
  London-based Dealogic plc 44
lenders
  rights and obligations
    sub-clause 96
lending banker
  options 141–142
LIBOR 102, 177
  level 102
loan agreement 89, 132, 178
  agent and lenders 115
  amendments 120
  categories 90
  conditions 97–98
  consents 120
  definitions 91–95
  facility
    lender's rights and obligations 96
    multi-currency term loan
      facility 96
  fees
    types 103–104
  guarantee 106–109
  interest rate 101–103
    sub-clauses 101
  law and jurisdiction
    Law Debenture Society 121
  legal opinions 121–124
    foreign exchange restrictions 121

novation
  draft documentation 116
obligors
  changes 119
other indemnities 105–106
preamble 90
prepayment
  borrower 100
  lenders 100
purpose 96–97
repayment
  types 98
sharing payments 116
taxes and other deductions 105
transfers of participations
  ways 116
undertakings 110–119
utilization
  drawdown of the loan 98
waivers 120
loan covenants
  drawbacks 128
  functions 125–128
  guidelines 129
  types 129–130
loan documentation
  guarantees 38
loan facility
  reborrowing
    revolving loan facility 100
Loan Marketing Association (LMA)
    49, 170
  achievements 155
  Barclays Capital 65
  committees 154–155
  future aims
    two-way communication 156
    straight-through-processing 156
  objectivies 153

Index

Loan Syndications and Trading
    Association (LSTA) 50, 146,
    148, 149
  activities 150
  committees 151–153
  corporate loans
    commercial banks 149
    private debt 149

majority bank 34, 178
  credit committee 35

negative covenants
  financial activities 140
non-financial covenants
  guarantees 130
  negative pledge 130

participants
  borrower 29
  capital adequacy
    capital adequacy ratios 15
  direct marketing
    efforts 13
  fee income
    London Inter Bank Offered Rate
      16
    see also LIBOR
    Praecipium 15
    syndication strategy 19
  market presence
    cross-border loans 14
  quality and spread of assets
    good customer base 13
    trade finance 14
  regulatory pressures
    Basle agreement 14
  responsibilities
    commitment 33

cross default 35
event of default 34
majority banks 34
payment sharing 35
secondary market sales 36
simplicity and speed
  credit decision 12
tax efficiency
  booking office 15
  'offshore' tax structure 15
project financing
  Export Credits Guarantee
    Department (ECGD) 80
  repayment phase 80
property loans
  types 84

ratings agencies
  Moody's 71
  S&P 71
reference banks
  screen rates 36
repayment profiles
  types 69
repayments
  bond issues/acquisition finance
    Euroloan market 72
  loan facility 70
  risk/return ratio 72
return on assets (ROA) 16, 19, 180
revolving facilities
  borrower
    short-term requirements 68
  commitment fee 68

secondary loan market
  history and development 146–148
  Loan Pricing Corporation (LPC)
    146

Index

International Swap Dealers Association, (ISDA) 148
Emerging Markets Traders Association (EMTA) 148
LSTA 148
secondary market sales
  assignment 36
  novation 36
secondary market 6, 36, 190
  uniform standards 146
SPV 7, 8, 77, 83, 180, 181
  borrower 77
syndicated loan market
  borrower 7
  British banks
    Barclays Capital 63
  credit ratings
    impact 164
  growth
    League tables 43
    merchant banks 2
  major players 43
  market-flex pricing 164
syndicated loans 1–2
  aircraft finance
    macro-economic factors 82
  arranger and the agent
    fee income 21
    market presence 21
    Megabank UK plc 22
    roles 37
  Asia-Pacific
    borrowers 57
    industry volume 62
    providers 53
    rankings 48
  credit rating agencies
    bank loan market 156
    'efficient' vs. 'inefficient' markets 157–159
    value-loaded analysis 159
    Sarbanes–Oxley Act 159
  EMEA
    borrowers 56
    industry volume 61
    providers 52
    rankings 47
  finance
    pre-export 75
    trade 75
  global
    borrowers 54
    industry volume 58
    providers 49
    rankings 45
  introduction
    single loan agreement 1
    syndicated lending market 1
  Jorf Lasfar Power Station 3
  'jumbo' loans
    France Telecom 5
    Vodafone plc 5
  key figures
    arranger and the agent 37
  medium-term loans 30
  mezzanine finance
    liquidation 73
  non-recourse loans
    SPV 83
  participants
    agent's role 37
    payment risk 36
    reference banks 36
  other market drivers 164
  pre-export finance
    features 75

Index

syndicated loans (cont.)
  project finance
    national infrastructure project 79
    private finance initiative (PFI) 78
    types 77
  property finance
    loan to value 84
    macro-economic reasons 84
  secondary market
    loan documentation 6
    trading methodologies 6
  senior debt
    customary type 73
  ship construction finance
    good standard 83
  standby credits
    corporate bond programme 83
    small commitment fee 84
  stock loans
    debunture 77
    SPV 77
    trade finance 76
  structure and purpose
    margin and fees 8
  structures 43, 66
    committed and uncommitted facilities 68–69
    currency 69
    evergreen facilities 72
    finance 75–76
    mezzanine finance 73
    repayment profiles 69
    repayments 70
    revolving facilities 68
    securitization 74–75
    senior debt 73
    stock loans 76
    subordinated loans 73
    term of loan 67
    subordinated loan
      shareholders 73
      quasi-capital 73
  tombstones 21
  US
    borrowers 55
    industry volume 60
    providers 51
    rankings 46
    Vodafone AirTouch 85
  syndications
    types 66

term loan agreement 125
term of loan
  Eurobond issue 68
  repayment period 67
tombstone
  Financial Times 22
transfer of participations
  conditions of transfer 117
  transfer fee 117
  procedure for transfer 117
  responsibility of lenders 117

undersubscribed loans
  unsuccessful syndications 19
underwritten transactions
  acquisition finance 66, 168
  arranged or best efforts 67
  club deals 67
US banks
  balance sheet availability 49

Vodafone AirTouch
  jumbo loans 88
  mobile phone 85

well-designed covenants
  performance indicators 128

LaVergne, TN USA
18 August 2010
193672LV00002B/12/P